Dylan Thomas's Swansea, Gower and Laugharne

Dylan Thomas's Swansea, Gower and Laugharne

JAMES A. DAVIES

www.uwp.co.uk

British Library Cataloguing-in-Publication Data
A catalogue record for this book is available from the British Library.

ISBN 978-1-7831-6003-7
e-ISBN 978-1-7831-6008-2

Typeset by Hewer Text UK Ltd, Edinburgh
Printed by CPI Antony Rowe, Chipenham, Wiltshire

Contents

Acknowledgements

For invaluable help of various kinds the author thanks Paul Ferris, Ann Heilman, Lorraine Scourfield, and the staff of Swansea Central Reference Library, West Glamorgan Archive Service and the libraries of University of Wales Swansea. The author is grateful to Susan Jenkins, Liz Powell and all at University of Wales Press who worked on the first edition of this book, for exemplary, friendly and enthusiastic professional attentions. This new edition owes much to Sarah Lewis of UWP. Needless to say, the author remains responsible for all errors and opinions in this volume.

The author and publishers gratefully acknowledge the permission granted by the following:

Extracts from Dylan Thomas, *Under Milk Wood* (1954; J. M. Dent/ Everyman, 1992); *Poet in the Making: the Notebooks of Dylan Thomas*, ed. Ralph Maud (J. M. Dent, 1968); *Early Prose Writings*, ed. Walford Davies (J. M. Dent, 1971); *The Poems*, ed. Daniel Jones, revised edn (J. M. Dent, 1982); *Collected Stories*, ed. Walford Davies (1983; J. M. Dent/Everyman, 1995); *The Collected Letters*, ed. Paul Ferris (J. M. Dent, 1985); *Collected Poems, 1934–1953*, ed. Walford Davies and Ralph Maud (J. M. Dent, 1988); *The Notebook Poems, 1930–34*, ed. Ralph Maud (J. M. Dent, 1989); *The Broadcasts*, ed.

Ralph Maud (J. M. Dent, 1991); *The Filmscripts*, ed. John Ackerman (J. M. Dent, 1995); *Under Milk Wood*, 'The Definitive Edition', ed. Walford Davies and Ralph Maud (J. M. Dent, 1995), reproduced by permission of the estate of Dylan Thomas, J. M. Dent, London.

US rights: Extracts from: *A Child's Christmas in Wales*, copyright © 1954 by New Directions Publishing Corp.; *Quite Early One Morning*, copyright © 1954 by New Directions Publishing Corp.; *The Collected Stories of Dylan Thomas*, copyright © 1954 by New Directions Publishing Corp.; *The Poems of Dylan Thomas*, copyright © 1952 by Dylan Thomas. Reprinted by permission of New Directions Publishing Corp.

D. J. Thomas (p. 4), Dylan and Nancy Thomas (p. 26), Dylan and Caitlin Thomas (p. 81), family group (p. 107), reproduced by permission of Jeff Towns, *Dylan's Bookstore* collection.

Florence Thomas (p. 27), reproduced by permission of Paul Ferris.

Daniel Jones (p. 12) reproduced by permission of Hulton Getty Picture Collection.

Castle Street (p. 50), Swansea Grammar School (p. 57), Bay View Hotel (p. 66), reproduced by permission of the West Glamorgan Archive Service.

'Warmley' (p. 42) reproduced by permission of Elizabeth Stead.

'Boat House' and St John's Hill (p. 90) reproduced by permission of Alan Shepherd Publishing.

'Eros' (p. 99) reproduced by permission of Kathy de Witt.

'Sea View' copyright © Colin Vosper.

Bethesda Welsh Baptist Chapel, Swansea copyright © Jaggery.

Cwmdonkin Drive (colour section p. 1), Dylan Thomas Centre (colour section p. 2), Bethesda Chapel (colour section p. 3), Dylan Thomas statue (colour section p. 4), interior of 'Work Hut' (colour section p. 5), Laugharne castle (colour section p. 6), 'Boat House' (colour section p. 8), reproduced by permission of Photolibrary Wales'

Acknowledgements

Every effort has been made to trace the copyright holders of material reproduced in this volume. In the case of any query, please contact the publishers.

Preface

DYLAN THOMAS WAS BORN in 1914. Of course, 2014 marks the first century since the year during which the First World War began, the war, it was thought, erroneously, that would end all wars. Since the late 1920s, when he began writing assured parodies in his school magazine, interest in Thomas's often notorious life has rarely flagged; his poetry, short stories and *Under Milk Wood* still attract the general reader as well as the specialized literary critic. His work has never been out of print. From the moment in the 1930s when he burst out of provincial obscurity to dazzle the London literary world, conquer North America and build an international reputation as a writer, to his early death – partly through alcohol – in a New York hospital, he became and has remained the archetypal bohemian poet, careless of money, personal reputation and conventional behaviour.

All legends simplify and Thomas's is no exception. This guide to the three places that were most important to him – Swansea, Gower and Laugharne – demonstrates the complexities of his life's geography. He could be, for example, very much the suburbanite, bourgeois at heart, a poet who has been brilliantly compared (by Anthony Conran in *The Cost of Strangeness*) to John Betjeman. And, for all his roistering, 'boily-boy' reputation, famous among the bars of London and New York, he also loved quieter places, where he could establish a routine and in which he wrote a number of his most famous poems. He found such places on Gower and, particularly, in Laugharne.

Biographies and studies of Thomas continue to be written, most recently by Andrew Lycett. An edition of his poems selected by the Irish poet Derek Mahon is another recent publication. A new and comprehensive edition of the complete works, to be edited by John Goodby, is also planned (and already financed). There seems no end to interest in Thomas's life and work

Thomas was also one of the most autobiographical of writers and so this book's other function is to show how real places enter his work, at times in a very detailed way. The present writer is very aware that because literature is not life and has a complex relationship with its realist material there is need to tiptoe warily through – or skate speedily over – the seductive quicksand of what used to be called the autobiographical heresy.

Finally, visitors must also be reminded that because Dylan Thomas had good cause to be a writer much possessed by rain they should never stray far from a good-quality umbrella.

Chronological Summary

1876	The poet's father, David John Thomas, born in Johnstown, near Carmarthen
1882	The poet's mother, Florence Williams, born in St Thomas, Swansea
1899	David John Thomas became English master at Swansea Grammar School
1903	30 December, David John Thomas married Florence Williams
1906	The poet's sister, Nancy Marles Thomas, born in Swansea
1914	Family moved into 5 Cwmdonkin Drive
	27 October, birth of Dylan Marlais Thomas
1925–31	At Swansea Grammar School
1931–2	Journalist on the local paper
1934	First visit to Laugharne
	18 Poems
1936	*Twenty-five Poems*
1937	11 July, married Caitlin Macnamara in Penzance Registry Office
1938	Lived at 'Eros', Gosport Street, Laugharne
1938–40	Lived at 'Sea View', Laugharne
1939	Birth of Llewelyn Edouard Thomas, their first son
	The Map of Love

1940 Stayed with John Davenport at Marshfield, near Chippenham
Portrait of the Artist as a Young Dog

1941–5 Worked in London as a scriptwriter for Strand Films and Gryphon Films

1943 Birth of Aeronwy Bryn Thomas, their daughter
New Poems published in the United States

1944–5 Lived in New Quay, Cardiganshire

1945–9 Lived in Blaen-Cwm, London, Oxford and South Leigh

1946 *Deaths and Entrances*
Selected Writings published in the United States

1949 Moved to the 'Boat House', Laugharne
Birth of Colm Garan Hart Thomas, their second son

1950 First American tour

1951 Lived for three months at 54 Delancey Street, Camden Town, NW1

1952 Second American tour, accompanied by Caitlin
In Country Sleep and Other Poems published in the United States
10 November, *Collected Poems 1934–1952*
16 December, death of David John Thomas

1953 Death of sister Nancy
April–June, third American tour
14 May, first performance, in New York, of *Under Milk Wood*
19 October, began fourth American tour
Further New York performances of *Under Milk Wood*
5 November, admitted to St Vincent's Hospital, New York, in a coma
9 November, death of Dylan Thomas, without regaining consciousness
24 November, buried at Laugharne

1954 *Under Milk Wood* published

1958 Death of Florence Thomas

1994	Death of Caitlin Thomas
2000	Death of Llewelyn Edouard Thomas
2009	Death of Aeronwy Thomas-Ellis
2012	Death of Colm Garan Thomas

I

Swansea – 'the best place'

Background – from Jack to 'D.J.'

IN 1899 A YOUNG man in his early twenties, from a Welsh-speaking, chapel-going, working-class family in Johnstown, then a village near Carmarthen, came to work in Swansea. That summer he had been awarded first-class honours in English by the University College of Wales, Aberystwyth, the only student of English in all three colleges to take a 'first' that year. He came to Swansea to take up a temporary post as an English teacher at Swansea Grammar School. His academic brilliance would have encouraged him to regard this appointment as a stepping-stone to better things, possibly to an academic post or, perhaps, to a position as an inspector of schools or director of education. He also had literary ambitions and was trying to publish poetry. But all his dreams faded. He got nowhere as a poet and, apart from a brief period at Pontypridd Grammar School during 1900 and 1901, he spent his whole career, until retirement in 1936, in the school to which he came in 1899.

This young man was David John Thomas, 'Jack' to his family, who became 'D.J.' the schoolmaster and Dylan Thomas's father. Coming to Swansea must have filled him with nervous excitement. Founded, so it was said, by a Viking named Sweyn, Swansea ('Sweynsei') was essentially a twelfth-century Norman creation, part of the Marcher Lordship of Gower. It became a place of strategic importance: the castle commanded the mouth of the River Tawe. Later it developed as a port and a market town that by the eighteenth century was mainly English speaking. In 1786 it was advertising itself as 'the Brighton of Wales', seeking to exploit the rising popularity of sea-bathing in order to reinvent itself as a fashionable resort. Assembly rooms, a reading society, circulating libraries and a theatre duly appeared. But genteel ambitions literally went up in smoke with the rise of metallurgical industries – copper smelting, particularly, plus zinc smelting and tinplate manufacture – fuelled by rich and easily accessible coal seams. Victorian Swansea became 'Copperopolis', 'Tinopolis' and the 'metallurgical capital of the world'.

By 1899 the town's industrial heyday had probably passed, but it was still a smoky, prosperous, sprawling place of works, factories and railways, a place 'rooted in heat and flames'. The town centre had narrow, bustling, cluttered streets, with chapels, churches, schools, theatres, cafes, restaurants and pubs, as well as fetid slums and alleys. When the wind blew from the east it brought factory smoke and smells. In the docks, which, in the years up to the Great War, continued to thrive and expand as the west Wales coalfield developed, ships disgorged hundreds of seamen into sleazy, sometimes violent pubs, brothels and cheap lodging houses. In the manner of all boom towns it continued to build monuments to its own magnificence. In 1899 *Ben Evans*, the huge department store, was barely five years old. It was followed by the head post office in Wind Street (1901), then the Harbour Trust Building (1903), the Glynn Vivian Art Gallery (1910), the Central Police Station (1913), and the Coal Exchange Building (also 1913). Swansea was not at all like Aberystwyth, let alone Johnstown. To David John Thomas, the young product of smaller and quieter places, it must have offered a cultural and environmental shock of seismic proportions.

The poet Edward Thomas, who had relations in the area and knew it well, wrote of being taken up 'to Town Hill . . . to see the furnaces in the pit of the town blazing scarlet, and the parallel and crossing lines of lamps, which seem, like the stars, to be decoration. If it is always a city of dreadful day, it is for the moment and at that distance a city of wondrous night.' The contrasts intrigued him: glimpses of the sea from 'sunless courts', the sooty town on the superb bay. He was fascinated by industrial Swansea. But he also noticed villas built around the bay and, to the west of the town centre where the prevailing westerlies kept smoke and grime away, the beginnings of middle-class suburbia.

By 1914, the year in which Edward Thomas's essay on Swansea appeared in the *English Review*, David John Thomas, now always 'D.J.' to his colleagues, despite increasing bitterness at what had become his professional lot, had established himself as a teacher of English. In 1903 he had married a local girl, Florence Williams, from the St Thomas area of Swansea's east side, on the edge of dockland. Her father, like D.J.'s, was a railwayman and, like D.J. himself, George Williams was from Carmarthenshire, in his case from the rural peninsula between Carmarthen and Llansteffan. His daughter Florence was a seamstress in a local draper's. On the face of it, this was a strange marriage for an ambitious, highly intelligent, professional man who was also something of a dandy and very conscious of his own dignity. Almost certainly, as used to be said, he 'had to marry her'; in 1904, their first child, which did not survive, was born in the small terraced house which the couple rented at the top of Sketty Avenue, then on the edge of farmland. Little more is known of their early married life; all else has vanished into the murk of Edwardian Swansea that, in its turn, has disappeared almost completely. But we know the marriage survived. A daughter, Nancy, was born in 1906, by which time they had left Sketty for more rented accommodation at 31 Montpellier Terrace and 51 Cromwell Street in central Swansea.

In 1914 Nancy was eight, and Florence pregnant. During the summer in which Britain declared war on Germany, D.J. moved his

David John Thomas. Dylan's father. His graduation photograph (*c*.1899–1900), academic cap worn jauntily, reveals a handsome young man confidently awaiting the success that never came.

family from Cromwell Street to become the owner of newly built 5 Cwmdonkin Drive in the expanding Uplands area of west Swansea. In doing so he became part not only of the expansion glimpsed by Edward Thomas but also of the fundamental change in Welsh society during the early years of the twentieth century: the appearance of a substantial middle class and of middle-class suburbia. Only in the larger places – the Radyr, Rhiwbeina and Roath Park areas of Cardiff, the Mumbles, Sketty and Uplands parts of Swansea, possibly in Newport – was it possible for that suburbia to emerge. In Wales, where quite often the professional man lived close to the manual worker – as, for instance, in the valleys of south Wales even into the 1950s – this was a wholly new social phenomenon.

Dylan Thomas's Swansea

Dylan Marlais Thomas was born on 27 October 1914 during, as he once said, the first battle of Ypres. His middle name came from his father's uncle, William Thomas, who wrote poetry and prose in Welsh under the bardic name of Gwilym Marles, taking the latter name, pronounced 'Marrless', from the Marlais stream near his birthplace close to Brechfa. William Thomas had been educated at the University of Glasgow, before becoming a Unitarian minister and schoolmaster in Cardiganshire whose turbulent inclinations led to eviction from his chapel for supporting tenants against landowners. He died in 1879, aged only forty-five. Socially and intellectually, Gwilym Marles was the family's high-flyer and D. J. Thomas was obviously proud of the connection. Daughter Nancy's full name was 'Nancy Marles Thomas'; it was said that her brother was named 'Marlais' because no one ever pronounced 'Marles' correctly.

In 1914 Swansea was a town (it became a city in 1969) with a population of about 100,000 divided fairly sharply between two areas. To the east around and beyond the river was industrial and working-class Swansea. To the west, where Dylan Thomas was born and grew up, was the generally prosperous, anglicized, mainly pious and comfortable, middle-class world. Indeed, the Uplands of his day has been described by the social historian Peter Stead as a 'sophisticated middle-class suburb, in which bards, ministers and academics were thick on the ground'. It was – and to some extent remains – self-contained, with a shopping centre, private schools, churches and chapels, parks, a cinema and respectable pubs and clubs. The town centre, Swansea Grammar School, the new University College, the county cricket and rugby ground at St Helen's, were all within walking distance or a short tram-ride away. As has been noted, like most of central Swansea it was predominantly English-speaking, particularly in Dylan Thomas's own generation. For D.J. and many like him Welsh belonged to the old, poor, rural world from which they had escaped, one that they certainly did not intend their children to inherit. The Uplands middle class, though, was essentially Welsh in that its occupational range was wider and its gradations different from, say, parts of Surrey – a schoolteacher, for example, probably had more social status in Swansea. And, like all such areas, it had its share of snobbishness and affectation: Paul Ferris, himself a Swansea boy, in his biography of Dylan Thomas, recalls the barbed joke that, in middle-class Uplands, sex was what coal came in.

As a grammar-school master teaching boys who, certainly in the early part of his career, were sifted socially through entrance examinations and fee-paying, with almost absolute power in the classroom and short working hours, D. J. Thomas enjoyed something of a gentlemanly existence. This was not, however, a source of contentment. He had few friends and was open in his disdain of both his work, which he thought beneath his intellectual abilities, and his less well-qualified colleagues. He was sharp-tongued, could be foul-mouthed and – perhaps significantly, given his son's fatal addiction – was a regular and sometimes heavy drinker. These were persistent working-class attitudes in a bourgeois world. He was also agnostic at a time of buoyant church and chapel attendance and, in a sober-suited world, he was something of a dandy. All such characteristics we might now understand as the consequences of being trapped in an unsatisfactory marriage and of the tensions of social mobility. Certainly he was never at ease, let alone content, in a world dominated by mortgagees with pretensions to gentility.

D.J. was not required to fight in the Great War and so carried on teaching. Meanwhile, Swansea's docks, railways and works boomed with the war effort, as did agriculture in west Wales. This was, though, the last flourish of the old world; the war was 'a massive watershed'. In 1918 and through the 1920s the town mourned and came to terms with the carnage of the Western Front. The Great War fascinated the young Dylan Thomas: one of his early memories was hearing of 'a country called "The Front" from which many of our neighbours never came back'. He wrote a number of school-magazine poems on the subject; one, 'Missing', about a soldier lying dead on a battlefield, was for the war's tenth anniversary in 1928, when the poet was fourteen. The war remained an important and, at times, explicit presence in his first two volumes of poetry, as, for example, in 'I dreamed my genesis', where he wrote of

> shrapnel
> Rammed in the marching heart, hole
> In the stitched wound and clotted wind, muzzled
> Death on the mouth that ate the gas.

Swansea was not immune to the effects of the slump that devastated much of Wales in the 1920s and 1930s. At its worst 10,000 of the town's workforce were unemployed and, in east Swansea, there were pockets of dreadful poverty. We catch glimpses of this in *Portrait of the Artist as a Young Dog*, the fictional recreation of 1930s Swansea, when Thomas describes the unemployed as 'silent, shabby men at the corners of the packed streets, standing in isolation in the rain', the scavengers along the railway lines, and the homeless 'tucked up in sacks, asleep in a siding, their heads in bins'. The then vicar of Swansea, Canon W. T. Harvard, all too aware of the town's abrupt social divisions, deplored the fact that 'one half of the world did not know how the other half lived'. This was a comment that could also have been directed at Dylan Thomas and his friends: they knew comparatively little of the east side.

Yet Swansea survived the Depression better than most Welsh places. Demand for anthracite coal and tinplate continued, which helped to keep the docks buoyant and service industries to survive. In Swansea's western suburbs it was domestic employment that helped to keep the wolves from many working-class doors. The Thomas family in its new semi-detached house was typical in employing a maid who lived in, as well as a regular washerwoman; Patricia, in Dylan Thomas's short story, 'Patricia, Edith, and Arnold', is based on one of the former.

Swansea between the two world wars was a lively place with its fine buildings, churches and chapels, theatres, cinemas, clubs, pubs, cafes, sports teams and newspapers. It was a powerful focal point not only for its own suburbs but for west Wales as a whole. This was Thomas's 'ugly-lovely' atmospheric town, crammed, for the most part, between hills and the magnificent sweep of the bay. It was, as perhaps it had always been, a frontier town where urban, English-speaking Swansea met the rural Welsh-language heartlands of west Wales and the Swansea Valley, and tried to keep its distance from urbanized but Welsh-speaking Llanelli. Within the town itself, the East Side and West Swansea created their own edgy lines of demarcation.

Swansea had two mainline railway stations, High Street and Victoria, the latter near where the present-day leisure centre stands, and other smaller ones. Until 1936 the town was also criss-crossed by tram routes. Tram-like carriages (the Mumbles train) still ran round the bay to Oystermouth, a small fishing village that had developed into a residential suburb that was also a centre for boating, sailing and holidays, and to Mumbles with its pier. The schizophrenic nature of the town persisted, not only between east and west but also, even more abruptly, between the solidly bourgeois commercial and shopping centre of High Street and Wind Street (always pronounced 'Wine Street') and the sleazy, sometimes violent, port district that included the Strand, in places less than twenty yards away from respectable streets. This juxtaposing of order and seeming chaos, of the familiar and the disorientating, this sense of being able to slip so easily from one to the other, all so vividly illustrated by the town's topography, often finds its way into Thomas's work and, strangely but tragically, into his personal life.

Even through the economically depressed 1920s and 1930s the town continued to expand. When Thomas was very young he had played in the fields above Cwmdonkin Drive, but in the late 1920s most of these disappeared under the Townhill Council Estate. Uplands and Sketty themselves continued to develop as transport improved and the inevitable westward drift away from polluted industrial areas took place. Such expansion, however, masked fundamental industrial decline. Copper smelting, and the many other associated metallurgical activities that had once been the vibrant basis of the town's prosperity, ended in 1921; by 1939 almost every local colliery had closed. Swansea was sustained by being a commercial and shopping centre, by a continuing iron and steel industry, the beginnings of the oil industry and through a still flourishing port. But it had long ceased to be a boom town.

By mid 1937 both children were married – Dylan to Caitlin Macnamara, despite parental opposition – D.J. retired and he and Florence had let 5 Cwmdonkin Drive (it was not sold until 1943). They moved to another semi-detached house in Bishopston, on the Gower peninsula. They stayed there until spring 1941 when German bombing of nearby Swansea forced them to Blaen-cwm in rural Carmarthenshire, where D.J. had inherited a small cottage. During the short period spent in Bishopston, Swansea had changed almost beyond recognition.

Industrial Swansea had a good war. Works and factories poured out munitions, and the docks were of great strategic importance. But for the town itself the war was a disaster. Because of the port's importance it was targeted by the Luftwaffe, which began attacking Swansea in 1940. The 'Three Nights' Blitz' of 19, 20 and 21 February 1941, seemingly intended for the docks, instead devastated forty-one acres of the town centre, killing 230, injuring 409, and making over 7,000 people homeless. Some 857 premises were destroyed or irreparably damaged. Dylan and Caitlin Thomas, visiting D.J. and Florence at Bishopston, saw it all for themselves on 22 February. Bert Trick, an old friend of Thomas's, met the couple in the ruined streets. 'Our Swansea is dead', Thomas said to Trick, and was close to tears.

In February 1947, during a bitter winter, Dylan returned to Swansea to research 'Return Journey'. He walked around the town making notes, and later he wrote to the Borough Estate Agent for the names of shops in vanished streets. The debris had been cleared and the roads reopened, but little or nothing had been rebuilt. Stopped clocks still showed the time the bombs fell.

'Return Journey' remains one of his most moving radio features, the marvellous humour intensifying the pervading sense of loss.

D. J. Thomas, for long in poor health, died in Laugharne in 1952. As is well known his son died in New York on 9 November 1953. Neither saw much of the reconstruction of central Swansea that began with the opening of the Kingsway in November 1950. That was perhaps just as well. The attractions of conservation, let alone of pedestrianization and shopping malls, belonged to the future. There was no attempt to recreate even the best of the lost buildings, and they were replaced by low-rise, blandly functional, concrete boxes. The medieval street plan that had given character to the town centre was now abandoned in favour of straight dual carriageways. Yet, despite that insensitive rebuilding and further development, what is remarkable is how much of Dylan Thomas's own Swansea has survived the planners, either actually or suggestively, not only in Uplands, Sketty, Oystermouth and Mumbles, which emerged from the war relatively unscathed, but also in the modern city centre.

Such survivals are in addition to what might be described as the commercialized persistence of the magical name. In Swansea East's Llansamlet, a part of the city of which he knew little, there is a Dylan Thomas Restaurant. In Oxford Street we find the Eli Jenkins Pub and Winebar, which would surprise *Under Milk Wood*'s unworldly clergyman, as would the pub sign, which transforms Llareggub's versifier into a bibulous Victorian squire. Also in the city centre, in Northampton Lane behind the YMCA, is a block of flats the name of which, Tŷ Caitlin, unexpectedly evokes that turbulent lady's home-making qualities. Not far away, in Sketty Park, is Laugharne Court, a council-run complex of sheltered accommodation for old people, the association of Laugharne with retirement suggesting that Dylan Thomas withdrew to his Sunset Home on the estuary while still in his mid-thirties. *Dylan's Bookstore*, owned and run by the indefatigable Jeff Towns, is in King Edward's Road, having moved from Salubrious Passage off Wind Street. Dylan's Wine Cellar is in

Dillwyn Road, Sketty; Dylan's Wine Merchant is in Gorseinon. All this is in addition to the Dylan Thomas Community School and Dylan Thomas house, 5 Cwmdonkin Drive, where Thomas was born and grew up. This last, owned privately, is available for visits and short stays.

Swansea was the greatest formative influence on Dylan Thomas, even though his knowledge of the town was limited. His Swansea was mainly the town centre, the middle-class suburbs and Oystermouth and Mumbles at the western end of Swansea Bay. He grew up in his comfortable though fraught home with his bitter, volatile, bookish father, his homely, cheery and indulgent mother, and his older, rather distant sister. His mother took him, perhaps dragged him, to chapels and their Sunday schools. He played in the park and on the sands, a small private dame-school close to his home prepared him very inadequately for grammar school. In English, if in nothing else, with some help from his father and much from his father's library, he prepared himself superbly for the great literary deeds that lay ahead. At grammar school he edited and contributed to the school magazine, debated, acted, won races, paid no attention to any subject except English, and left as soon as he could for a brief, inglorious career as a local journalist. His father, the senior English master feared by pupils and colleagues alike, seems to have stood, or fumed, idly by.

Dylan's first intellectual awakening came not in school but through his friendship with Daniel Jones (1912–93). This gave him access to Jones's Sketty home, still named 'Warmley', full of books, music and culture and, importantly, congenial company and a welcoming atmosphere, these last two qualities, in particular, seemingly in shorter supply in his own home. The two boys made their first ventures into serious writing and composing, and began to formulate literary and musical ambitions. Jones – who became a distinguished composer whose work included thirteen symphonies, No. 4 in memory of Dylan Thomas – was the closest of a group of lifelong Swansea friends, a number of whom shared similar

Daniel Jones, Thomas's closest friend and a member of the Kardomah group, who died in 1993. Jones remains one of Wales's most distinguished composers.

aspirations. They also idled away part of their youth in cafes, and in pubs through beery evenings that ended with sustaining fish and chips or breath-disguising cachous as they swayed home to warm beds in drowsing, respectable streets.

To young middle-class men brought up in pre-war Uplands and Sketty, working-class Swansea, particularly the industrial east side and dockland, could seem like a foreign land whose natives might be occasionally observed, as they are in Thomas's writings. In 'One Warm Saturday' a group from Brynhyfryd enjoys itself in the saloon of a pleasure boat to Ilfracombe; on Saturday nights in High Street, Thomas wrote in 'Old Garbo', 'sirens from the Hafod sat in the steaming chip shops with their handbags on their knees and their ear-rings rattling'. Daphne, the grass widow in Manselton who is Mr Roberts's downfall in 'Where Tawe Flows', as well as those Hafod sirens, remind us that, viewed from middle-class Cwmdonkin, the east side seemed, if not to seethe, at least to flutter with sexual promise.

This last intensified Thomas's sense of lower-class Swansea as a place of chaotic darkness into which respectable members of the middle class could quickly slide, as in 'Old Garbo', when young Thomas and Mr Farr's pub crawl takes them all too rapidly from the respectable 'Three Lamps Hotel' in Temple Street to a sleazy pub in the Strand, and in 'One Warm Saturday', which ends with the young narrator losing his girl and himself in a tenement block somewhere in St Thomas. To repeat, schizophrenic Swansea becomes an uncanny reflection of Thomas's own wildly oscillating life.

At times, of course, there may be some artistic licence in his treatment of his home town or, to put it another way, the use of conscious or unconscious symbolism. Certainly, during his brief career as a local journalist that preceded the writing of the *Portrait* stories, Swansea East became less mysterious. In 'Return Journey', for instance, he laughs at his farcically inexpert reporting of bouts at the Mannesmann Hall, once an important boxing venue near the Mannesmann tinplate works. Both hall and works have dwindled into the name of a turning off the Plasmarl bypass, in what used to be Swansea's industrial heartland.

It is too glib simply to say that Dylan Thomas was the product of familial genes. But when we recall Gwilym Marles's opposition to landowning authority and D. J. Thomas's simmering resentment of his suburban lot, we may be indicating one source of the young man's instinctive hostility to a seemingly repressive environment. But that real hostility would come later. For Thomas the child, his world was a place of wonder: 'Never was there such a town as ours'. It offered a potent combination of street, park, beach and sea, of a doting mother, of Christmases recalled as warm Dickensian celebrations, and of friends, gangs and rivalries.

Like all children the young Dylan had a hidden life of the imagination, even though his was more intense than most and certainly better remembered. His secret literary life began in the late 1920s. In public he was the school magazine poet, writing astonishingly assured parodies, humorous verse and conventional lyrics about the Great War. In private he embarked on different adventures with words. With Daniel Jones, he wrote strange poems in which each wrote alternate lines, creating effects that were often surreal and sometimes beautiful. Collaborations were followed, in his mid-to-late teens, by the notebook poems, intense, often sexual, and known only to close friends like Jones. At the same time he was writing letters to friends old and new and to editors of magazines to which he sent poems.

Here are lively literary beginnings in congenial company. If we add acting with local amateur groups of good quality, the high-spirited social life of young men with few responsibilities and a first job as a journalist soon relinquished for creative leisure in a comfortable family home, we might wonder what he could possibly complain about. But the young man was haunted not only by the need to write but also by the desire to conquer the wider literary world. In the semi-autobiographical *Portrait* short story, 'The Fight', inspired by a visit to what is obviously his friend Daniel Jones's home, he glimpses 'the future spread out beyond the window . . . and into smoky London paved with poems'.

Given this yearning for more spacious horizons, a recurring theme in his notebook poems and early letters is his attitude to Swansea. The young writer explores the problems of living in what he felt to be 'the smug darkness of a provincial town' with, he told Pamela Hansford Johnson, 'unutterable melancholy blowing along the tramlines'. From the same period of his life emerge first drafts of 'I have longed to move away', and the more menacing 'Ears in the turrets hear', in which the poet fears a hostile world and wonders what to do. The sentiments of these two poems, reflecting what Thomas felt to be provincial, suburban, middle-class repression inimical to creativity in general and literature in particular, echo through works written after he had escaped. In the *Portrait* story, 'Where Tawe Flows', for example, it is difficult not to see Thomas himself endorsing Mr Evans's view of suburbanites existing 'under the shadow of the bowler, like you and me'.

Inevitably, as he grew older and life became more difficult, his views changed. The later critical comments are invariably linked to qualifying positives, not only the famous 'ugly-lovely' reference, but also the 'stained and royal town' of 'Holiday Memory', the 'beautiful drab town' of a letter to Charles Fisher, and 'the dizzy ditchwater town at the end of the railway lines' of the late short story, 'The Followers'. Swansea is recalled, increasingly, as a place where happiness once was and could – perhaps . . . perhaps . . . still be grasped. He wrote, again to his old Swansea friend, Charles Fisher: 'Swansea is still the best place . . . I'll set up . . . in a neat villa full of drinks and pianos and lawnmowers and dumb-bells'. To Vernon Watkins, he described Swansea as his 'marble-town, city of laughter, little Dublin'. To Daniel Jones he wrote of impossible hopes of returning to Swansea to found, with his friends, 'a permanent colony' that would recapture the spirit of his Swansea upbringing.

Thomas may have left for London in 1934, but he was always returning. In one sense, of course, he has never left, for his presence can sometimes be sensed in odd moments in places where once upon a time he could be found. Rain sweeping into a deserted Cwmdonkin Park from a Swansea Bay where foghorns often drone, old facades and pre-war remains above modern shop-fronts in High Street and Wind Street, the sound of drinkers in those famous Mumbles pubs: in such moments 'in and out of time' we might almost expect to encounter, even now, the 'bulging apple' that was Thomas in his prime, still, to adapt Vernon Watkins's words, striking sparks from Swansea streets and making the windows burn.

Dylan Thomas and Swansea's literary history

'Of all the cities and towns of Wales,' wrote the late Sir Glanmor Williams, once the doyen of Welsh historians, 'Swansea has a history unsurpassed in length, importance, variety, and interest'.

Dylan Thomas's knowledge of that general history was probably limited, but that of Swansea's literary history was another matter. During his short-lived career as a local journalist, when he worked for the *South Wales Evening Post* and its associated weekly newspaper, *The Herald of Wales*, from 1931 to 1932, he wrote six articles in the latter paper on writers with local connections. Five discuss 'The Poets of Swansea', and one (see chapter 2) explored 'A Modern Poet of Gower'. The articles on Swansea cover the period from the 1790s to the First World War and necessarily – and, perhaps surprisingly, apologetically – are restricted to those who wrote in English.

Thus Thomas excludes what are, in the city's literary tradition and within his timescale, important Welsh-language moments. One was the founding of the first Welsh-language newspaper, *Seren Gomer*, which began in Swansea in 1814 and astonishingly survived, mainly as a Baptist quarterly, until 1983. Secondly, Swansea was a source of sad inspiration for William Thomas ('Islwyn', 1832–78), the Welsh-language poet from Ynysddu in Monmouthshire. His fiancée, Anne Bowen, who died suddenly, and Martha Davies, the woman he later married, were both from the town. Islwyn's love for the former dominated his marriage to the latter, creating a strange tension that fuelled his finest poetry. Thirdly, 'Calon Lân', the famous hymn and erstwhile rugby anthem written during the 1890s, is Swansea's greatest contribution to Welsh hymnology: the words are by Daniel James of Treboeth and the music by John Hughes of Landore. Two other distinguished writers of Welsh have strong Swansea connections: William Crwys Williams (1875–1968), triple winner of National Eisteddfod Crowns and Archdruid of Wales, was for many years a minister in Brynmill; Saunders Lewis (1893–1985), perhaps the most distinguished of all twentieth-century Welsh-language writers, lectured at what was then the University College of Swansea from 1922 to 1937 (he was dismissed for helping set fire to an RAF bombing school in Caernarfonshire, as a nationalist protest).

For Thomas, all such moments – to mix a metaphor – were a closed book. That same volume also, it seems, included literary links with Swansea earlier than the 1790s. Thus he had nothing to say about Daniel Defoe (1660–1731), who was impressed by Swansea despite scepticism about the healing reputation of local mineral waters, and said as much in his *Tour Through the Whole Island of Great Britain* (1724–6). Neither does he mention Richard Savage (*c.*1697–1743), who came to Swansea from London in 1739 to escape debts and enemies. Savage lived for two years in a house in Barber Court off Orchard Street, a site later occupied by the Kingsway roundabout. Some insist that his Swansea poetry includes an accomplished celebration of Hafod, the inner city area that still bears some of the scars of the copper works that once dominated the district. The poem, whether or not by Savage – which opens

> Delightful Hafod, most serene abode!
> Thou sweet retreat, fair mansion for a god!

– reminds us that Hafod (in English, 'summer place'), improbable though it now seems, was once a beauty spot and favourite walk. Nor does Thomas mention William Combe (1741–1823). From 1809 Combe became famous for the verses he wrote to accompany the caricaturist Thomas Rowlandson's illustrations in a series of books chronicling the adventures of Dr Syntax, a grotesque clergyman. Combe spent the period 1769–73 wandering the provinces pursued by debts and scandals. He was sighted in Swansea 'as a waiter at an inn', the old Mackworth in Wind Street, doubtless gathering material for his later success. (Rowlandson (1786–1827) visited Swansea in 1797, making several drawings of the area; in his opinion Caswell Bay was 'the finest sandy beach I ever saw'.)

With one exception, Thomas's articles are concerned with poets, which probably accounts for the exclusion of E. A. ('Amy') Dillwyn (1845–1935), literary critic for *The Spectator* (where she was one of the first to praise *Treasure Island*) and novelist whose fiction included *The Rebecca Rioter: A Story of Killay Life* (1880). Thomas does, however, refer to Thomas Bowdler (1754–1825), George Borrow (1803–81), and Edward Thomas.

Bowdler completed *The Family Shakspeare* (1818) while living in 'Rhyddings House' in Brynmill, and is buried in Oystermouth churchyard. His 'merciless editorship' of Shakespeare, as Dylan Thomas puts it, which struck out all perceived profanities and indecencies, immortalized the editor in the verb 'to bowdlerize', meaning 'to expurgate'. Surprisingly Thomas is sympathetic towards the famous mangler. It is easy to scoff, he wrote, but it is also possible to agree with Swinburne, who considered that Bowdler helped to popularize Shakespeare by making 'it possible to put him into the hands of intelligent and imaginative children'. George Borrow, the well-known travel-writer, came to Swansea when working on *Wild Wales* (1862). Thomas comments that Borrow entered through Landore, referred to as 'Glandwr', which he found very muddy, and he quotes Borrow's general, and less than flattering, description of Swansea as a 'large, bustling, dirty, gloomy place'. But, Thomas notes with some satisfaction, 'he praises the ale'. As for Edward Thomas, whose essay on Edwardian Swansea has already been quoted, in this article Thomas says only that he spent some time in Waun Wen, staying with the headmaster of the local school.

The account of 'the poets of Swansea' begins in earnest with Walter Savage Landor (1775–1864), an eccentric and unjustly neglected writer of fine prose and beautiful lyrics and the original of Boythorn in Dickens's *Bleak House*. In 1796, during Swansea's 'Brighton of Wales' period, he was living in 'Rhyddings House', still to be found, sadly reduced, on the corner of Bernard Street and St Alban's Road in Brynmill, the house that Bowdler would occupy a few years later. Thomas describes one of Swansea's most famous literary moments, Landor's meeting with the young Rose Aylmer that resulted in 'one of the most beautiful and most popular short poems in the language':

Ah, what avails the scepter'd race,
  Ah, what the form divine!
What every virtue, every grace!
  Rose Aylmer, all were thine.

Rose Aylmer, whom these wakeful eyes
  May weep, but never see,
A night of memories and of sighs
  I consecrate to thee.

Thomas, though slightly misquoting, praises the dignity and strict economy of these lines: this was 'great poetry in every sense of the word; not a phrase, not a word, could be altered to its advantage'. Landor, he insists, is not to be described as a local poet but as one of 'national, international' standing.

Thomas offers a long list of Swansea poets before concentrating on a small number. Ann Hatton, 'Ann of Swansea', the sister of Sarah Siddons, despite her consistently mediocre verse, is recognized as Swansea's first author with a public reputation. Samuel Palmer Chapman was a poor poet but a sincere one. Others – J. C. Manning, C. D. Morgan, John Evans, H. A. W. Rott, and E. E. of the enigmatic initials, all now forgotten – are generally dreadful, even though Manning offers odd moments of beauty. They are disposed of in a single article.

'Mr S. C. Camwell', who was, in actuality, Samuel Clearstone Gamwell ('Camwell' is an error), writing under the witty nom de plume of 'Pierre Claire', has an article to himself. He edited *The Cambrian*, Swansea's leading newspaper before *The South Wales Morning* [later *Evening*] *Post.* Yards of verse on local themes and events appeared in his paper, 'marking the parish-pump with the hands of the true journalist'. Thomas pays tribute to the common sense that strengthened Camwell/Gamwell's influence on local opinion exerted through that prolific versifying.

The fifth article is on James Chapman Wood who, as a writer with a London publisher, was a cut above most other

Swansea poets. His first collection, *A Child of the People*, was published in 1879 by Kegan Paul. Thomas considers that he wrote good poetry, poetry of technical merit and intellectual force, engaging with life around him. Ultimately, perhaps, Woods's poetry is too serene and too derivative, but his work has 'an essential sanity' and lines of great beauty. His best book, *A Pageant of Poets*, is a series of eulogies on his great predecessors. Thomas concludes that because he took from the great he can be linked to them, even though he was hardly great himself.

One local figure above all captured Dylan Thomas's imagination. He was Llewelyn Prichard (Thomas Jeffery Llewelyn Prichard (1790–1862)), the subject of article two, 'a genuine figure of fancy' with a 'strange and disordered' life. Prichard was born in Breconshire and died in 'World End Cottage' in Swansea's Thomas Street. Prichard, who was for some years an actor and always a prolific writer of poetry and prose, was the author of *Twm Shon Catti* (1828), the eponymous hero of which, a kind of 'Welsh Robin Hood', remains one of the most memorable characters in Welsh literature. Prichard's life fascinated the young Dylan Thomas. Having lost his nose in a duel, a replacement wax nose made him look ridiculous and the butt of children. During his years in Swansea he lived for a time in Wassail Square (now covered by the Quadrant Shopping Centre) before jeering children drove him to Thomas Street. He had become a drunkard who (shades of later Dylan Thomas!) once lost a whole volume of his work in the Red Cow Pub in High Street. A collection was made to keep him out of the workhouse. It was not necessary: one night in 1862 he came home drunk, fell asleep over his papers, a falling candle set his room alight and he died in the fire. 'He failed to be great', Thomas writes, 'but he failed with genius.'

'The Poets of Swansea' tells us much about Dylan Thomas and his home town. He was only seventeen when he wrote the articles; and the extent of his reading is at the very least impressive. Possibly he was assisted by his father's book collection, more probably by the town's libraries. Either way the articles are a tribute to the young man's capacity for self-education. Thomas not only read his way through the local writers and distinguished visitors but was also able to place them in a wider literary context. Thus, Matthew Arnold's statement that literature should be a 'criticism of life' is used as a touchstone, and influences and borrowings – Milton, Scott, Wordsworth, Byron, Mrs Hemans, Hopkins, are among the references – are confidently detected. He shows a detailed knowledge of literary history – he has even read Sidney Colvin's study of Landor – and of leading poets from the Romantic period into the twentieth century.

Thomas is scathing about poor poetry but unexpectedly charitable if any writing of quality can be found. The articles demonstrate the extent to which he was proud of, immersed in and thus influenced by his Swansea milieu. They also reveal much about the young man's thinking on literary matters. Apart from his endorsement of Arnold's view of literature, implicit in all the articles is the need for a poet to find a fresh, personal voice, the important distinction between local and universal, and the desirability of having a London publisher. Such views surely reflect the young writer's still-hidden ambitions. Sadly anticipatory, however, is the extent to which the young Dylan Thomas is attracted towards Llewelyn Prichard's tragic life. Prichard typifies larger-than-life literary figures who step away from routine living to become 'men stepping on clouds, snaring a world of beauty . . . half wild, half human . . . Prichard stands out flaming and aloof against the horizon'. In such hero-worship of the disorderly bohemian life are the seeds of Thomas's eventual calamity.

In the 1930s Thomas himself, with Vernon Watkins, and his other friends, the lesser figures of Charles Fisher and John Prichard, together with Wynford Vaughan-Thomas, continued Swansea's literary history into its golden age. Even after his death, his literary presence has continued to affect the course of that history. John Ormond (1923–90), the most considerable Swansea poet to follow Thomas and Watkins, struggled, with eventual success, to keep Thomas's influence at bay. More recently, the still-vibrant tradition has become essentially reactive, as two examples demonstrate. Kingsley Amis (1922–95), who lectured for ten years at the University College, satirizes Thomas and his work through the characters of Gareth Probert in *That Uncertain Feeling* (1955) and Brydan in *The Old Devils* (1986). A group of Swansea poets who came to prominence in the 1960s and 1970s – including Bryn Griffiths, Graham Allen, Alan Perry, John Beynon, and Peter Thabit Jones – in the main attend to an East-Side world and a working-class Swansea of which their famous predecessor knew little.

Dylan Thomas's Swansea – Cwmdonkin, Uplands and Sketty

CWMDONKIN

'Cwmdonkin' is an odd name. Once, apparently, it was 'Cwmdawkin', which combined a common Welsh word for a narrow valley or hollow with what may well be a reference to the Dawkin family, who in the 1720s lived in what is now Sketty Hall and probably owned the land. Nobody knows why the name changed, if indeed it did. Somehow it seems fitting that a name so strongly associated with Dylan Thomas should combine word play with a decently intriguing level of obscurity.

Thomas called 'Once it was the colour of saying' his 'Cwmdonkin poem'. It describes the area as 'the uglier side of a hill', presumably because urbanized, as distinct from the fields above Cwmdonkin that until the late-1920s extended over Townhill. In *Adventures in the Skin Trade* Cwmdonkin Drive (thinly disguised as Mortimer Street) and the district as a whole stand for the stultifying suburbanism hated by Samuel Bennet, the story's anti-hero and, as has been seen, feared by the young Dylan

Thomas. Even in 'A Child's Christmas in Wales' Cwmdonkin, covered in snow, is a 'chilly glinting hill', more hostile than welcoming. In the comic poem, 'The Countryman's Return', Thomas describes himself satirically, but, as ever, with a careful eye on class distinction, as

> A singing Walt from the mower
> And jerrystone trim villas
> Of the upper of the lower half

But, as always with Thomas, his reactions were ambivalent: 'Holiday Memory', written in 1946, contrasts the comforting permanence of home with insubstantial pleasure. Returning from the fairground on a warm August bank holiday night, 'as we climbed home, up the gas-lit hill, to the still homes over the mumbling bay, we heard the music die and the voices drift like sand'.

Despite his sometimes fierce protests, Thomas was very much at home in middle-class suburbia. As he admitted to Vernon Watkins, he belonged to 'the bound slope of a suburban hill, the Elms, the Acacias, Rookery Nook, Curlew Avenue . . . the aspidistra, the provincial drive, the morning café, the evening pub'. He liked, as he put it in 'Poet: 1935',

> Leaning from windows over a length of lawns,
> On tumbling hills admiring the sea[.]

His suburbanism feeds into his writings and is one of his strengths. Even at his most grandly rhetorical he never wholly loses touch with ordinary language. Not for nothing has he been compared to John Betjeman.

CWMDONKIN DRIVE

Even by the standards of a town built on hills, Cwmdonkin Drive is a steep street. The Rhondda writer, Gwyn Thomas, once wrote that Rhondda hills had such severe gradients that many who watched the first cars struggling to climb them during the 1930s were convinced that Henry Ford had backed a loser. The inhabitants of Cwmdonkin may well have thought the same. Often, even now, let alone before the era of the car, the hill is alive with the sound of heavy breathing. Drinkers had the predictable additional problem: 'The revolving hill to my father's house reached to the sky', laments the drunken narrator in 'Old Garbo'. When Thomas famously described himself as 'the Rimbaud of Cwmdonkin Drive', thus neatly combining poetry with debauchery, he did so in defiance of the slope.

Near the bottom of the Drive is Richmond Road, the beginning of a horseshoe that, as Hillside Crescent, reconnects with Cwmdonkin Drive. The Grant-Murrays lived at 17 Richmond Road; Thomas played with their children and helped build Guy Fawkes bonfires on an open space behind their house. Cwmdonkin Drive is one-sided. On the other was

> a capsized field where a school sat still
> And a black and white patch of girls grew playing.

The school was Clevedon College, a small private school, mainly for girls, occupying a large house in treed grounds that were sometimes grazed by 'coughing sheep . . . [that] plague my life'. Trees and sheep preoccupied the young writer, and they are prominent in 'Upon your held-out hand', the notebook poem written in June 1932. When he was seven, he writes, he counted forty-four trees; now he thinks of a thousand sheep, numbered to counter insomnia. The school has gone, as have many of the trees and all the sheep, to be replaced by Clevedon Court, a cluster of modern houses with its own entrance into Cwmdonkin Park that continues Swansea's western drift. Further up the Drive is a small, enclosed reservoir, the remains of a larger one that once extended into Cwmdonkin Park. Immediately opposite the reservoir is Dylan Thomas's birthplace.

5 CWMDONKIN DRIVE

In 5 Cwmdonkin Drive, to echo famous words, we begin at the beginning. He was born in the front bedroom of what is one of a pair of semi-detached houses, built in 1914, about halfway up the steep Drive, on the right-hand side. A blue plaque commemorates the association. Since it has preserved its original bay windows – an expense of wood in a waste of UPVC, to adapt the words of a famous sonneteer – plaque apart, in appearance it has changed little from Thomas's day. As has been noted, this was the Thomas family home until 1937. After the house was sold in 1943 a series of occupiers included Emlyn Davies, who became known as an illustrator of Thomas's poems. The house is now privately owned and, at the time of writing, offers conducted tours and literary events.

The narrow frontage is deceptive, for the house has much depth. Its 'front' door is at the side, leading into a hallway from which access is gained to the three main ground-floor rooms. The front room, overlooking the Drive, was the parlour, kept for special occasions; it has the original fireplace and a stylish moulded ceiling. The middle room was D.J.'s study, with his desk (now in the 'Boat House' in Laugharne), some Greek statuettes and an extensive library described by his son as containing 'nearly everything that a respectable highbrow library should contain', by which he meant the classics plus reference books, and books about literature. During D.J.'s day the study had a separate rear entrance and exit, which doubtless allowed him to escape quietly to the pub. At the back of the house is a living room leading to a large kitchen and scullery and a back door opening on to a small yard and garden. In the still extant wash-house the washerwoman worked every Monday for two shillings and sixpence plus a meal. Upstairs were four bedrooms and a bathroom. On 27 October 1914 Dylan Thomas was born in the large main bedroom at the front of the house, a room usually kept 'for best'. Sister Nancy slept in the next room, adjoining the bathroom. Addie Elliott the maid, from St Thomas, who was paid

Taken on Swansea Bay sands *c.*1920; teenage sister Nancy poses, 6-year-old Dylan considers mischief.

six shillings a week and her keep, had the small box-room on the other side of the bathroom. Thomas's parents slept in the large, bay-windowed bedroom at the back. When a growing second child necessitated rearrangement, Thomas appears to have taken over the maid's tiny room. He described it in a letter: '*Very* tiny. I really have to go out to turn round . . . Hot water pipes very near. Gurgle all the time. Nearly go mad. Nice view of wall through window.' There he kept his own books, mainly of modern poetry: the list he gave Pamela Hansford Johnson ranged from Hopkins, Stephen Crane and Yeats, through Owen and Sassoon, to Auden, Lawrence and the Sitwells. In that small room Thomas read voraciously, filled the famous *Notebooks* and wrote his first published poems. This is now a second bathroom.

A study in middle-class homeliness: Florence Thomas, Dylan's mother, *c.*1934, when she was 52, in the living-room of 5 Cwmdonkin Drive.

When sister Nancy married and left home in 1933, Thomas may have moved into the back bedroom, once used by his parents, with its bay window affording views over town and sea. His short story, 'The Orchards', begins in this room: Marlais the young writer, blocked and sexually frustrated, steps out of the window and walks across the roofs of the town, then westward to a picnic in a field with two inviting sisters. The story dramatizes the power of upbringing and sexual disappointment; both may well have been linked.

The eight years gap between Nancy and Dylan meant that the arrival of the second child – and a son – caused great excitement. The midwife recalled that D.J. celebrated too well and returned home unable to take off his own boots. All too soon, since the baby at first slept in a cot in his parents' bedroom and was not a placid child, D.J.'s initial delight gave way to fury at being disturbed. But there was a positive side: even when his children were very young he read Shakespeare to them, presumably believing in a kind of improving osmosis. His mother believed her son to be 'delicate', possibly asthmatic; certainly his bones broke easily. She spoiled him dreadfully. In the autobiographical short story, 'Patricia, Edith, and Arnold', the character of the boy, aged about four or five, may well catch much of what young Thomas was like: observant, knowing, provocative, used to having his own way, something of 'a handful', as they used to say.

From 5 Cwmdonkin Drive the young boy was taken to his first school. When almost eleven he walked to and from Swansea Grammar School on every school day. After leaving school in 1931 and working for fifteen months as a local journalist, he settled into a home routine reminiscent of a Wodehouse novel with his mother as Jeeves. In a letter to Pamela Hansford Johnson he described it as 'Night and Day: A Provincial Rhythm'. This began with breakfast in bed (his mother even took the tops off his boiled eggs) between half past nine and ten o'clock each morning, when he also read the newspaper and had a leisurely cigarette. The rest of the morning was spent reading in front of the fire, before he strolled down the hill for one or two pints of beer in the Uplands Hotel, returning home for lunch and an afternoon of reading, writing or walking. Evenings were often spent in pubs in Mumbles or elsewhere, or at drama rehearsals when Thomas became a member of the Swansea Little Theatre. The day ended with a walk home for supper and late-night reading and writing. 'Not a very British day', he commented ruefully and perhaps guiltily, 'Too much thinkin', too much talkin', too much alcohol.' But, despite familial tensions, mainly created by his father's temper exacerbated by beer, and, occasionally, by his son's school performance and later lifestyle, it was a very comfortable existence.

Perhaps significantly, Thomas's account makes no mention of friends calling on him. Some did, of course, and it was not unknown for Thomas, in his father's absence, to chat to his friends in his father's study, the parlour presumably being out of bounds. But such evenings were not frequent. D.J.'s bitterness, his unpredictable temper, his gloominess, tended, as Daniel Jones felt, to make the house a less than congenial place to spend time even with the closest of friends. Like his father, Thomas worked in his room after high tea and then went out. During his late teens they may have seen comparatively little of each other.

Thomas's relations with his sister were distant at best. She was much older and had her own life although, for a short time, they were both members of Swansea Little Theatre. Her letters to Haydn Taylor, a salesman who left Swansea for London and became her first husband, describe a household in which D.J. was always in a temper and where her mother steamed open her letters. She believed, with good cause, that her brother often stole money from her. Behind the respectable frontage of No. 5 was disturbed family life that would have interested Strindberg.

As if home life was not a sufficient trial, Thomas, true to his class-bound suburban instincts, was also uneasy about where he lived. In letters to Pamela Hansford Johnson, he refers to 'my nasty, provincial address' and, with heavy irony, to No. 5 as 'a small, not very well painted, gateless house . . . Very nice, very respectable.' However, when he wrote to Wyn Henderson, who lived in Cornwall, and was a more up-market friend with whom he had a brief affair, No. 5 became 'a mortgaged villa in an upper-class professional row', an odd mixture of indiscretion and snobbish inaccuracy.

As one might expect, 5 Cwmdonkin Drive features in a number of Thomas's writings, as has already been seen in the quotation from 'Poet: 1935'. In 'Ears in the turrets hear' his home is a refuge: a beleaguered young writer, apprehensive about what the world has in store, sees 'Ships anchor off the bay', hears hands that 'grumble on the door' and the wind and the rain beating against the house. 'I have longed to move away' is even more troubled:

Thomas longs to leave Swansea but is afraid. Meanwhile time passes, dramatized in the poem by the view from his home across the Mumbles end of the bay where 'the day / Goes over the hill into the deep sea'. No. 5 features in three *Portrait* stories: in 'Patricia, Edith, and Arnold', as has been seen, it is where the small boy plays before being taken to the park; 'Lavengro', the house where the writers' group meets in 'Where Tawe Flows' draws some details from No. 5; towards the close of 'Old Garbo', it is where young and hung-over Thomas cannot face his Sunday lunch after his Saturday night out with Mr Farr.

In 'A Fine Beginning', the first part of *Adventures in the Skin Trade*, Samuel Bennet's parents' house in Mortimer Street, with its family photographs, china and tea cosies, and marked school essays awaiting return, is closely based on Thomas's home. Samuel vandalizes the contents before leaving for London in a final, irrevocable gesture against his upbringing. Yet, once again, elsewhere Thomas offers a very different view of his boyhood home. No. 5 is the setting for most of 'A Child's Christmas in Wales', the famous magical synthesis of all his festive memories. In this account the boy is enraptured or puzzled by presents while his aunts and uncles crowd the house. The former drink home-made wine or port, the latter smoke new cigars in the front parlour. His parents are not mentioned. Snow falls outside, in defiance of mild Swansea's meteorological statistics.

'A Child's Christmas in Wales' ends on a comforting note: the boy gazing from his bedroom window on Christmas night, seeing, under the moonlight and against the snow, the lights of other houses 'on our hill and hear[ing] the music rising from them up the long, steadily falling night'. In 'The Peaches', the opening story of *Portrait*, the boy waiting for his uncle outside a pub, thinks longingly of 'the warm, safe island of my bed, with sleepy midnight Swansea flowing and rolling round outside the house'. Memories of home, particularly in Thomas's later, turbulent life, were ultimately comforting.

TO SKETTY VIA CWMDONKIN PARK

Near the top of Cwmdonkin Drive, on the left, is Cwmdonkin Terrace where young Thomas and his gang of friends once rang doorbells and disappeared smartly. Here was invaluable early training for success as a teenage athlete. At the very top of the Drive is a road junction. To the right is Terrace Road, leading, eventually, to Swansea Grammar School. To the left is Penlan Crescent, which has a number of entrances into Cwmdonkin Park.

Cwmdonkin Park

The park is not large and seems to hide away behind the Uplands. The entrances are unobtrusive. When entering from Penlan Crescent the visitor looks down steep slopes and through mature trees. It is a beautiful urban oasis mainly used by parents with young children, footballing youngsters and decorous (occasionally not-so-decorous) courting couples.

At one end is a bowling green and tennis courts with a small pavilion and shelter, much as in Thomas's day. Close by is the very same drinking fountain – part of it, at least – that he knew as a boy and in which he sailed his toy ship. The base still stands but the fountain is now waterless: the chained cup from which the children drank was an early casualty in the hygienic wars.

The bandstand that Thomas knew has also been removed, and the reservoir on the park's Cwmdonkin side has been filled in. On the latter is a children's playground and a grassy space for games. A Dylan Thomas memorial shelter, given by a local private school, is nearby. Thomas also played with his toy ship in puddles on the path from the drinking-fountain to the park's main entrance. In the notebook poem 'Rain cuts the place we tread' he complained that leaves often impeded sailing. That path now passes the Dylan Thomas memorial. This memorial is a medium-sized block of blue pennant stone from Cwmrhydyceirw quarry, in the northern part of Swansea, on which the sculptor and artist Ronald Cour has carved the last three lines of 'Fern Hill'. It is behind railings and surrounded by water. The project was financed by Caedmon Records of New York, whose owners, Barbara Holdridge and Marianne Mantell, had made the famous recordings of Thomas reading his own work. Dedication took place on 9 November 1963, the tenth anniversary of Thomas's death. Two lyric poems by Vernon Watkins, 'At Cwmrhydyceirw Quarry' and 'Cwmrhydyceirw Elegiacs', are meditations on choosing the stone. Watkins also played a leading part both in organizing the memorial and in the dedication ceremony. During the latter, moved by the occasion, he read at length from Thomas's work, superbly oblivious to the rain. The memorial has been incorporated into a water garden created in 1974 to mark Cwmdonkin Park's centenary. Unfortunately, the garden now tends to overwhelm the stone.

High above the park are the buildings of what was Swansea Teacher Training College, now part of Swansea Metropolitan University. The college's tendency to be hidden in low cloud is noted in 'Patricia, Edith, and Arnold'. According to some reports, in pre-war days the female students were a byword for daring behaviour (see page 83). Beyond the park, over the roofs of Uplands houses, is Swansea Bay.

Dylan Thomas was not the first writer to celebrate the charms of Cwmdonkin Park. Samuel Clearstone Gamwell, to whom, as we have seen, he gave prominence in 'The Poets of Swansea', wrote 'Don't Joe; Don't!', witty verse about courting couples, which opens:

At the Uplands Park
Ere leaf and bark
Are hidden from sight in the Night's black cowl
You may often hear
In the tree-tops near
The whirring notes of the Spinner Owl
Its purring noise
The heart decoys,

Like the chanting of Pussy at evening meal,
Or a homely rhyme
Of the olden time
When the maidens sat plying the busy wheel.
But I've sometimes heard an odder bird
Sing: 'No – I – won't!'
(Then, after a rustle, as if of a tussle):
Don't Joe; don't!'

Four similar stanzas follow; Gamwell was no minimalist.

Thomas on Cwmdonkin Park is more impressive. He remembered it all his life and it is a frequent presence in his writings. It enters four *Portrait* stories. The climax of 'Patricia, Edith, and Arnold', when the two housemaids meet and attack two-timing Arnold, takes place in the shelter around the bowls pavilion. Tom, unhappily married to the wrong girl in 'Just Like Little Dogs', often spends the night in the park, listening to the owls. Young Thomas, camping at Rhosili in 'Extraordinary Little Cough', thinks of life carrying on in seemingly far-off Cwmdonkin and the park. At the close of 'Old Garbo', teenage Thomas, post-prandially fragile after a night spent pub-crawling, and 'knowing that [he] will never drink again', sits alone near the bandstand, befriends a stray dog and begins a very bad poem which he later destroys. In 'Reminiscences of Childhood', the park was 'a world within the world of the sea-town . . . full of terrors and treasures . . . a country just born and always changing'. 'Return Journey' ends, movingly, in the park full of snow. The narrator recalls 'the childish, lonely, remembered music fingering on in the suddenly gentle wind'. The park-keeper was John Smallcombe, known as 'old Smally'; his portrait, resplendent in uniform, is part of the permanent Thomas collection in the Dylan Thomas Centre. When he is asked whether he remembers the narrator when young he replies with a long description of the boy playing in the park, leading to the famous and chastening conclusion: 'Oh yes, I knew him well . . . I've known him by the thousands.'

Cwmdonkin Park is an equally frequent presence in the poetry. 'Rain cuts the place we tread' has already been noted. 'See, on gravel paths under the harpstrung trees', the notebook poem revised as 'Poet: 1935' and published in *The Herald of Wales*, uses much park detail (swans on the reservoir, for instance) as a setting for youthful angst. More of this last is in the notebook version of what, much revised and reduced, became 'Not from this anger'.

> I sit and mark
> Love wet its arrow in the park

writes the young poet, seemingly slighted in love, surrounded by post-Gamwell couples intent on 'catching the moment's honey'. 'The first ten years in school and park', written when Thomas was eighteen, is, however, concerned more with the former than the latter, though 'hopes dead as mown grass' may be a lugubrious use of the symbolism of park maintenance. The park features strongly in two important early poems – 'Especially when the October wind' with its 'star-gestured children', and 'Should lanterns shine', with its well-known closing lines:

> The ball I threw while playing in the park
> Has not yet reached the ground.

Two famous Thomas poems use the park as a symbol of childhood invaded by a darker adult world. The first is 'Once it was the colour of saying', written in 1938 and, to repeat, described by Thomas as his 'Cwmdonkin poem'. In it he recalls a time when he

> whistled with mitching boys through a reservoir park
> Where at night we stoned the cold and cuckoo
> Lovers in the dirt of their leafy beds.

The second is 'The hunchback in the park', revised in 1941 from a notebook draft of 1932. Thomas writes of a real-life hunchback who came regularly to the park in the early 1930s, staying all day despite the shouts of 'truant boys', and fantasizing about a beautiful woman who might remain there through every night, after

> the wild boys innocent as strawberries
> Had followed the hunchback
> To his kennel in the dark.

Even Cwmdonkin Park, it seems, was not forever idyllic.

In the *Portrait* story 'The Fight', fictional young Dylan, on his way to his friend Dan Jenkyn's home in Eversley Road, Sketty, exits from the park through the main gates into Park Drive. As he walks he recites his poems aloud to the empty street, ceasing quickly to prevent embarrassment when a couple emerge from a 'black lane'. Park Drive leads to Glanmor Road, where Kingsley Amis once lived, and, eventually, to the junction with Sketty Avenue.

Ahead is Tycoch, above which is Cefn Coed Psychiatric Hospital, which opened in December 1932. It is described by Thomas, in a letter to a friend, as 'like a snail with the two turrets of its water towers two snails' horns'. In the notebook poem 'Upon your held-out hand',

> The new asylum on the hill
> Leers down the valley like a fool.

Sketty Avenue was, of course, where Thomas's parents lived when they were first married. Their son may have known this. He would almost certainly not have known that in their first home his mother lost the child the conceiving of which probably forced them into marriage. At the bottom of the steep Avenue is Eversley Road. After turning left at the junction, 'Warmley',

Daniel Jones's old home, is a few yards down the hill on the left hand side.

TO SKETTY – VIA UPLANDS

The young boy rushing through the gate of 5 Cwmdonkin Drive could have walked a different way to Sketty. To do so he would have walked down the Drive past Richmond Road and Cwmdonkin Close, then, perhaps, through Uplands Terrace.

First left off the Terrace is Mirador Crescent. At No. 22 – now, like most of the area, divided into flats and bedsitters – was the small private school, in reality a 'dame-school', kept by Mrs Hole, which Thomas attended until he was ten. Fees were £10 per annum. Though Thomas later claimed that he was taught to read and count, in fact he learned little and was over-indulged. If he was reprimanded for bad behaviour – and he was, from all accounts, a very badly behaved little boy – he complained to his mother who visited the school in a rage. He became the archetypal teacher's pet. In some ways Mrs Hole's school was the worst kind of educational and social beginning; in others it was invaluable in fostering the solipsistic independence of spirit that made him the writer he became.

In an early letter to Pamela Hansford Johnson he refers to his 'preparatory school' where he first encountered 'Tobacco (the Boy Scouts' enemy)'. In 1943, in 'Reminiscences of Childhood', the school is recalled fondly as 'firm and kind and smelling of galoshes'. In 'Return Journey', redolent with a lost life, memories of practical jokes are overwhelmed by 'the distant, terrible, sad music of the late piano lesson'. In the lane behind the school, the 'lane of confidences', he learned to smoke and led the boys in urinating 'God save the King' on a convenient wall. At least to the age of ten, this last was one of his most considerable school achievements.

Uplands Terrace connects with the main road from the city; at this point it becomes Uplands Crescent, which passes Gwydr Square. Trams from the town centre heading for Sketty once ran through the Crescent, but they have long given way to the traffic jams of impatient commuters to and from the city centre. Yet, despite the sometimes fatal attractions of the outer suburbs, let alone of hypermarkets and out-of-town shopping malls, Uplands – always 'the Uplands' to Swansea folk – remains a lively place. It has retained its shopping centre, post office, some banks, churches, chapels and a pub. It is, though, no longer a traditional middle-class area. Most of the larger houses are now in multiple occupation, broken up into flats and bedsitters often occupied by students or young professionals, plus some ground-floor businesses and doctors' and dentists' surgeries with their crowded, apprehensive waiting-rooms. The presence of many foreign students gives the area a cosmopolitan edge; the small supermarket tends to stock a shelf or two of the comparatively exotic.

When, in 'Return Journey', that ubiquitous source, Thomas toured the haunts of his Swansea past, some of his most intense memories crowded upon him when he reached the Uplands. Even now, standing in Gwydr Square, we too can sense presences from Thomas's day. It is still possible, for instance, to identify with characters in the *Portrait* story 'Who Do You Wish Was With Us?', which begins in the Square on a beautiful summer morning in the early 1930s, long before heavy traffic. The narrator is a lightly fictionalized teenage Dylan. His companion, Raymond Price, troubled by unhappy memories of family deaths through tuberculosis, is based closely on Trevor Hughes, an early friend. Hughes was ten years older and lived in long-demolished Gorse Terrace with his widowed, invalid mother. He had literary ambitions that his friend encouraged but which came to nothing.

The two young men observe the families, well-dressed children, young men in flannels, and girls ready for the beach, the hum and bustle of a lively middle-class suburb on a holiday, as they begin an intended 15-mile walk to Rhosili by following Uplands Crescent past the Square.

This last connects the main road with Gwydr Crescent, which, in turn, out of sight of the main road, runs into Glanbrydan Avenue. At No. 69, Bert Trick, Thomas's communist friend and mentor, once kept a grocer's shop. Thomas and other friends, sustained by jelly and sandwiches, would meet in the living room behind the shop for informal and fiercely left-wing political discussion that 'threatened the annihilation of the ruling classes'. The evenings are recalled affectionately in 'Return Journey'. In that same room Trick's infant daughter Pamela once asked 'What colour is glory?' The question so intrigued Thomas that he used it in notebook versions of 'Why east wind chills', before it found a permanent home in 'My world is pyramid', the penultimate poem of *18 Poems* (1934), Thomas's first volume. The Tricks and grocery are long gone from the corner shop; the ambience remains. Opposite is Brynmill Park where, it is said, Thomas's parents once secretly met a pharmacist friend to receive medication for their son's gonorrhoea, this last possibly in 1935, after Thomas's first stay in London. Glanbrydan Avenue is on the edge of Brynmill, where Arnold, the two-timing boyfriend and chastened villain of Thomas's short story 'Patricia, Edith, and Arnold', thought Edith worked, only to discover, too late, that she was employed by Patricia's next-door neighbour.

The Rhosili-bound pair would have walked past the Uplands Hotel where D. J. Thomas once drank and where his son became the most regular of regulars. Then it had a front 'public' and a rear 'saloon', which, each evening, in D.J.'s day, catered for respectable, dark-suited, mainly professional family men popping out for a pint. In the 1980s it became a theme-pub called 'Streets', the theme being 'Dylan Thomas', with a circular central bar. Small, windowed rooms opened off the main drinking area, one of which was called 'Polly Garter's Pantry'. This dreadful example of cultural vandalism, which would have taxed even Thomas's capacity for satire, has been immortalized in Kingsley Amis's *The Old Devils*: the elderly visitors, blasted by rock music, sit in deck chairs on gravel floors and under beach umbrellas. The pub has since been reinvented as the Uplands Tavern, a more conventional establishment but retaining the central bar. A small plaque marking the Dylan Thomas association can be seen over the double door at the front of the building.

Fifty yards further up the Crescent, at the entrance to The Grove, is Lloyds Bank's Uplands branch. On this site, before the bank, was the Uplands Cinema, the local 'flea-pit'. Vernon Watkins, who as a child lived in posh Eaton Crescent, on the Swansea side of the Uplands, celebrates 'going to the pictures' in the days of melodramatic silent films in his poem 'Elegy on the Heroine of Childhood (in memory of Pearl White)'. A few years after Watkins, though still before 'talkies', Thomas and his friends were regulars. Some said that Thomas occasionally bought his ticket with money stolen from charity boxes. Certainly he fortified himself with wine-gums stolen from Mrs Ferguson's shop, then opposite the cinema in the road to The Grove, before graduating to purloined cigarettes. At times he demonstrated the ultimate in pre-teenage decadence, a small boy sprawling on the cinema's dilapidated plush seats while smoking a stolen cigar.

These boyhood visits to the Uplands Cinema fostered a lifelong interest in film and in cinema-going. The assured essay that Thomas wrote on 'The Films' in *Swansea Grammar School Magazine* during 1930 reflects serious thought about the medium. In retrospect it seems inevitable that he became a film scriptwriter. From

1941 until 1945 he wrote scripts for Strand Films and its successor, Gryphon and, for a short time after the war, he worked for Sydney Box at Gainsborough. On 28 October 1953, only twelve days before he died, he took part with Arthur Miller and others in a Cinema 16 Symposium in New York, making a perceptive point about poetry and the visual. As might be expected, film imagery is an important presence in his work. It can be found, for example, in 'The tombstone told when she died' and in 'Then was my neophyte'. In 'Our eunuch dreams' Thomas uses film as one example of unreal experience, the other being the dreams of adolescence. Both, the poem insists, should be set aside in order to confront and celebrate actual living.

Behind Lloyds Bank and between Nos 4 and 7, The Grove is Ebeneser Newydd (Y Llannerch). In 1949 this was still the BBC's Swansea recording studio. Here, on 24 October of that year, Dylan Thomas chaired a broadcast discussion on 'Swansea and the Arts'. The panel members were Vernon Watkins, Daniel Jones and the writer John Prichard. The producer was John Griffiths, who wrote the 'Griff and Tommy' children's books. 'Five of us', Thomas announced in his introduction, 'sit in this deserted Grove, on chairs, not hillocks.' He may have been delighted to know that the Dylan Thomas Society has held meetings in this building. At the end of The Grove is another entrance into Cwmdonkin Park.

Young Thomas and Raymond Price leave the Uplands along Sketty Road. Shortly after the right turning into Glanmor Park Road and opposite Parc Beck, is a large detached house named Glanrhyd, an early name for 5 Cwmdonkin Drive. Here we enter a different short story: 'I live in "Glanrhyd"', young Dylan tells his new friend in 'The Fight', for Dylan Thomas himself, one suspects, a revealingly pretentious moment. After Parc Beck is the main entrance to Singleton Park, the largest of Swansea's urban parks, once the grounds of Singleton Abbey, home of the Vivian family, the metallurgical barons. The abbey is now part of the university. The park, Thomas wrote, was 'crowded with lovers messing about'.

On the west side of Singleton Park is Sketty Green. Nearby was 'Rhyd y Helig House', long demolished and replaced by the small Rhyd-yr-Helyg housing estate. In 1933 the house was the home of Mrs Bertie Perkins, wife of a Swansea businessman, who allowed Swansea Little Theatre to perform Sophocles' *Electra* in the garden, with music by the young Daniel Jones. Thomas attended and, shortly after, published 'Greek Play in a Garden' in the *Herald of Wales* newspaper.

On the Sketty Road boundary of Singleton Park, at the junction with De la Beche Road (always pronounced 'Beach' and so Swansea's rejoinder to the famous geologist, Sir Henry de la Beche, who changed his name from 'Beach' for snobbish reasons) is St Paul's Church, Sketty, built in 1850 to commemorate a dead Vivian wife. It is 'shaking its bells for me', thought young Thomas, once again in 'The Fight', as he walked to Sketty.

In 'Who Do You Wish Was With Us?' young Thomas and Raymond Price walk on to Sketty Cross with its shopping centre and pubs. The Bush Hotel on the Cross was one of D. J. Thomas's occasional haunts. A grammar school colleague, J. Morgan Williams, recalled encountering him there, drinking alone, and he noted that the locals called him 'professor'. The same short story offers a brief and tantalizing glimpse of George Gray, fictional young Thomas's eccentric acquaintance. Londoner George, a 'cat's doctor', was paid to sleep with a policewoman still wearing her uniform; every morning he went to Sketty 'to help a woman put her clothes on'. At this point, the walk to Rhosili that is the central event of the story moves out of this Swansea chapter and into Gower.

'WARMLEY'

In 'The Fight', schoolboy Thomas, having reached Singleton Park, would have turned right into Eversley Road. Number 38, still called 'Warmley', was Daniel Jones's family home. Today there is nothing on this substantial property to mark the connection except for those who recognize the house-name at the front. When Thomas first came calling this was a spacious, relaxed and cultured home for a musical and artistic family who expected much from its brilliant son.

'Warmley' became Thomas's second home. He visited frequently and punned from afar on the house name, notably in a well-known emotional letter to Daniel Jones from Ireland in 1935, when Jones was living in Harrow. The letter, to quote Paul Ferris, is 'in memoriam for the "WARMDANDY-LANLEY-WORLD" as he calls it', knowing that it will never return. It was a world of boyish fights, cushion battles, and

'Warmley', 38 Eversley Road, Daniel Jones's aptly named boyhood home where Thomas was a frequent visitor. Much of 'The Fight' is set here.

cricket in the small back garden. They tried their hand at painting and sculpture. They played fantastic games during which they invented, as Daniel Jones recalled, a 'whole mythology of composers, instrumentalists and singers' with fantastic names. They constructed a radio station in the house, using loudspeakers, called Warmley Broadcasting Company, on which they – mainly Dan – performed their own music, and both tried out poems and short plays. They criticized each other's musical and poetic compositions. Most importantly of all, for Thomas, they collaborated in the writing of poems, calling the author Walter Bram ('bram' being Welsh for 'fart'). In this, as in most things, Jones took the lead; his range of reading and cultural experience was much wider than Thomas's and the latter learned much from him. The character of their friendship and their meetings in 'Warmley', lightly fictionalized – Jones, for instance, becomes Jenkyn, Dan Jones's middle name – is described in 'The Fight', most of which is set in the house. It is a story about two gifted youths preparing themselves for and dreaming about the beckoning future, the narrator sharing Thomas's own dream of, to repeat the quotation, conquering 'smoky London paved with poems'.

Dylan Thomas's Swansea – city centre

THE DYLAN THOMAS CENTRE TO THE GRAMMAR SCHOOL

The Dylan Thomas Centre is in Somerset Place. Built in 1825–9 it is described in the Glamorgan volume of *The Buildings of Wales* as 'the noblest classical building in Swansea'. This was once Swansea's Guildhall, then the annexe of Swansea Further Education College. After falling into disrepair it was completely reconstructed behind the preserved facade in 1993–4, to become the National Centre for Literature in 1995, when Swansea hosted the UK Year of Literature and Writing. It became the Dylan

Thomas Centre in the same year. The Centre contains a superb permanent exhibition of Dylan Thomas editions, manuscripts, memorabilia, and supporting material, collected by Jeff Towns. There is also a bookshop (new and second-hand) that is a branch of Jeff Town's *Dylan's Bookshop* in King Edward's Road, a small theatre/cinema/lecture hall, conference rooms, and a restaurant and bar. The public spaces exhibit reproductions of famous photographs etc., of Dylan Thomas and his world, and it is here that the annual Dylan Thomas Festival is based.

The Dylan Thomas Centre is on the edge of the Maritime Quarter. The latter, which belongs mainly to the 1980s, is based on the development of the old South Dock as a yachting marina surrounded by new and expensive apartment blocks. Dylan Thomas would not recognize the area and certainly would not recognize himself as the figure seated on a chair that is the Dylan Thomas sculpture by John Doubleday – bronze, 1984 – at the centre of Dylan Thomas Square. The piece catches the heaviness of Thomas in his last years, but the facial likeness is poor; the chair is excellent. The final lines of 'Fern Hill' are carved on the statue's base. At one side of the Square is the Dylan Thomas Theatre, the headquarters of the Swansea Little Theatre, with which Thomas acted during the 1930s. Then it was based in a church hall in Southend. A mural on the outside of the theatre has a youngish Dylan gazing past his statue, perhaps anxious to avert his eyes. Across a walkway near the Pump House Restaurant is a slightly mannered statue by Robert Thomas of Captain Cat, the blind sea-captain in *Under Milk Wood*.

Somerset Place runs alongside the Dylan Thomas Centre towards the city. At the junction with Adelaide Street is the handsome baroque building that once housed the Swansea Harbour

Trust. In 'A Fine Beginning', the first part of *Adventures in the Skin Trade*, dead Mr Baxter once worked here; his widow lives next door to the Bennet family in Mortimer Street.

Somerset Place connects with Quay Parade, the main road. To turn right is to pass Sainsbury's and cross the River Tawe (the old Mackworth Hotel, we are told in 'Return Journey', had beer like 'half-frozen Tawe water'). On the east side of the river is St Thomas, now a spruced-up area of small terraced houses cut off from the docks by the Fabian Way dual carriageway. Delhi Street runs parallel to Fabian Way. Thomas's mother, Florence Williams, was born in 29 Delhi Street in 1882, the youngest of seven children. Her parents had moved here from the Llansteffan peninsula in Carmarthenshire, from a rural family too many of whom gained reputations as heavy drinkers. Her father became a deacon in nearby Canaan Congregational Chapel, once near Maesteg Street off Foxhole Road, now demolished. As has been stated, Florence met her future husband when she was working as a seamstress for a local draper.

From St Thomas came most of the uncles who slept off the turkey and pudding in the parlour of 5 Cwmdonkin Drive, remembered in 'A Child's Christmas in Wales', as well as Auntie Dosie, who resorted to aspirin. George Hooping, the odd small boy in 'Extraordinary Little Cough', sometimes stayed in St Thomas 'with an aunt who could see through the walls'. Adjoining Delhi Street is Sebastopol Street: in 'Old Garbo', 'Katie Sebastopol Street' sings the national anthem in 'The Lord Jersey' pub. It is one of the streets over which the boy flies in 'Reminiscences of Childhood', as is Inkerman Street. As will be seen, in 'The Followers' Leslie and his narrator friend follow Hermione through an Inkerman Street misplaced in the town centre.

At the eastern end of Delhi Street is St Thomas's Church. Viewed from the higher parts of St Thomas, from, say, Grenfell Park Road where it passes above Maesteg Park, the church's tall spire is still silhouetted against the cranes and gantries of Swansea Docks. According to Ralph Wishart ('Ralph the books') this was the inspiration for Thomas's poem, 'The Spire Cranes'. In the poem, it must be said, the 'cranes' are birds.

Swansea Docks are still active and important but no longer the dominant presence of Thomas's day that made for frequent references in his writings. 'Ships anchor off the bay', he writes in 'Ears in the turrets hear', referring to those waiting for the pilot to take them into port. The wind from the docks tears up the street in 'Old Garbo'; in 'Return Journey' it slices through a wintry Swansea in which most windbreak buildings have been flattened by bombing and clearance. The sounds of seagulls from the docks are heard in 'A Child's Christmas in Wales'. In 'One Warm Saturday', Mr O'Brien and his car full of tipsy people drive from the pub past the 'still droning docks' on the way to Lou's room somewhere, it seems, in the St Thomas area. 'Holiday Memory', broadcast in 1946, recalls the 'sun-dazed docks round the corner of the sand-hills . . . the calling docks'. Young Thomas's fascination with the sea's romance – 'the dock-bound ships or the ships steaming away into wonder and India, magic and China', so often watched by those with nothing else to do – and the docks spread out beneath the flying boy, both contribute to 'Reminiscences of Childhood'. In 'Return Journey' we learn that young Thomas also watched 'the tankers and the tugs and the banana boats', and hoped to run away to sea. Only occasionally are there darker associations: we learn in 'Old Garbo' that a lip was once found outside the Missions to Seamen in Harbour Road: 'it had a small moustache'. Since he met her, he told Pamela Hansford Johnson with romantic cunning, 'the docks or the oven' are no longer options. In the *Portrait* story 'Just Like Little Dogs', the docks disappear.

At the junction of Somerset Place and Quay Parade was a subway (now filled in) leading to Wind Street. To the right of Wind Street, roughly parallel with it and connected by narrow lanes, is the Strand. As the name suggests it was once close to the river; it moved further away after 1852 when dock building necessitated a river diversion. In Thomas's day it continued above Wind Street, running behind the Castle, Castle Street and High Street and, as the Upper Strand, past Dyfatty, and Greenhill where the Irish once lived, as far as the Hafod. Although its notorious heyday had gone it was, as has been noted, still one of Swansea's worst areas, with its slums, sleazy pubs and lodging houses, and prostitutes, plus dockland businesses and workshops, some industry and the railway. During the 1930s the town mortuary was 47 Arches, Strand, and local journalists would often call there in search of newsworthy deaths. New, young reporters were always taken there as a rite of passage: in, once again, 'Return Journey', the Old Reporter recalls that young Thomas 'went pale green, mun', at his first sight of a corpse. The mortuary, and 'Jack Stiff', the mortuary keeper, feature in 'Old Garbo' and 'Just Like Little Dogs'. In the latter the narrator thinks of homeless scavengers laid out 'beyond pickings on Jack Stiff's slab near the pub'. Very little has survived German bombing and subsequent clearance and redevelopment. A few old buildings near Quay Parade, and here and there further up, still suggest something of the area's lost character.

It is possible that the teenage Thomas went to the Strand in search of prostitutes. Nothing is certain. Kent Thompson, an American who wrote a valuable doctoral thesis on Thomas's early life, records that Thomas and his friends were once chased out of the Strand because they were too well dressed. These good middle-class boys were horrified when an aged prostitute said to them, 'I only want a pint, boys, and I ain't got disease'. Bravado muffles truth, but that anecdote may well be true.

Nothing so earthy enters the fiction. 'Old Garbo' is the short story most concerned with the Strand and is centred on the Fishguard Arms. Now demolished, this was at 29 Strand, above Castle Lane and behind present-day Castle Street. Thomas, the cub reporter on the *South Wales Evening Post*, visits the pub with Mr Farr, his hard-bitten senior, who promises the somewhat bizarre: 'you can see the sailors knitting there in the public bar'. In the snuggery they meet 'Jack Stiff' from the mortuary. They also meet Mrs Prothero, Old Garbo herself. Her friends believe her daughter and baby have both died in childbirth, and they make a collection for her which she quickly spends on drink before it is discovered that her daughter is still alive. Mrs Prothero, unable to face the music, throws herself off the river bridge and is drowned. The presence of knitting sailors, plus the appearance of Ted Williams, an effeminate fellow reporter, suggests the Fishguard may well have been a gay rendezvous. If so, young Thomas would not have been a reliable witness: in 'Old Garbo' too much rum is seen to confuse recollection. Near the Fishguard Arms was the fictitious Fishguard Alley, probably Castle Lane, where, the narrator of 'Just Like Little Dogs' tells us, 'the methylated-spirit drinkers danced into the policemen's arms'.

Wind Street, less than a stone's throw from the sleazy Strand, was always highly respectable. In 1802 it was 'handsome and well paved' and led to the fashionable Burrows where Landor saw Rose Aylmer. By Thomas's day it had become the commercial heart of Swansea. However, what Hitler's bombs failed to accomplish the breweries have achieved with ease, turning fine, sometimes grand buildings into theme-pubs of amazing tackiness. In 1939 and living in Laugharne, Thomas recalled draughty Wind Street nostalgically in a letter to Charles Fisher, as a place where he longed to have 'smuts in my eye'.

1. *A Suburban Address: 5, Cwmdonkin Drive, Dylan Thomas's birthplace, his home for more than twenty years*

2. *The Dylan Thomas Centre, Somerset Place. Behind the preserved façade of Swansea's old Guildhall the city celebrates its most famous son.*

3. *Bethesda Welsh Baptist Chapel, Swansea. For years a grand expression of Nonconformist power. Dylan responded to its size.*

4. *The poet would not recognize himself: the Dylan Thomas statue in the Maritime Quarter's Dylan Thomas Square.*

5. *Dylan Thomas's work Shed, Dylan's Walk, Laugharne, where he wrote through most afternoons. Though only a recreation it still offers a brief and moving glimpse of his writerly life.*

6. *Laugharne Castle today. In the gazebo on the castle wall to the right Richard Hughes wrote* In Hazard *and Dylan Thomas* Portrait of the Artist as a Young Dog.

7. Sea View, Laugharne. This was Augustus John's 'doll's house'

8. The 'Boat House', Laugharne, Dylan Thomas's home from 1949 until death in 1953. The setting's beauty and tranquillity was a poignant contrast to the increasing turbulence of his domestic life.

Half way up Wind Street, on the left-hand side, is Salubrious Passage, an atmospheric covered alleyway with pillars, leading to Salubrious Place. Here, in what is one of the oldest parts of Swansea, was *Dylan's Bookshop*, for second-hand and antiquarian books. Its owner, Jeff Towns, is known internationally as the pre-eminent dealer in Dylan Thomas material, books, manuscripts and memorabilia. As has been noted, his magnificent private collection forms the permanent exhibition in the Dylan Thomas Centre. A friend of Thomas's named Alban Leyshon, a craftsman in metals, once had a workshop above the passage. The two would sometimes amuse themselves by dropping red-hot pennies from the window so that unsuspecting passers-by would burn their fingers. In Thomas's late story, 'The Followers', Salubrious Passage becomes 'Paradise Alley' and then 'Paradise Passage'. The former is where fat Mrs Penelope Bogan lives, the subject of Leslie's mildly lascivious recollection; through the latter the narrator and Leslie follow a 'stringy' girl who walks 'like a long gym-mistress' and whom they name 'Hermione Weatherby'.

'The Followers', published and probably written in 1952, is the only one of Thomas's Swansea stories to abandon coherent topography, here by using the Passage to connect Inkerman Street in St Thomas (see page 45) with what appears to be St Helen's Crescent (see page 63), here called 'St Augustus Crescent'. Next door to the Passage is the 'No Sign Bar' with a notice stating – a safe assumption – that Thomas was a frequent customer.

At the top of Wind Street is Castle Street and Castle Square. Here is what Thomas called, in 'Return Journey', 'the fragment of the Castle'. First mentioned in 1116, this was once the seat of the Lord of Gower. Then, it commanded the river. The ruin's main feature is a fine fourteenth-century arcaded parapet similar to those on the bishops' palaces at St David's and Lamphey in Pembrokeshire. In front of it is Castle Square. Until the blitz of 1941, this was the site of *Ben Evans & Co. Ltd* in Castle Bailey Street. 'Ben's' was Swansea's biggest and best department store. Gwyneth, one of the girl campers in 'Extraordinary Little Cough', is described 'as

Pre-war Castle Street. The Kardomah is the tall building on the left (opposite second lamp-post up). That side of the street was completely destroyed.

immaculate and unapproachable as a girl in Ben Evans' stores'. The shop is recalled in 'Return Journey' as being near to the Three Lamps Hotel, then in Temple Street (in full, 'Temple of the Muses' Street, because of the presence of the Theatre Royal, Swansea's first full-size theatre), where Thomas was once to be found 'lifting his ikkle elbow'. In 'Old Garbo', fictional young Thomas begins his pub crawl with Mr Farr in the back room of the Three Lamps. While he waits for the older man he drinks in the company of respectable professional men, wishes his father could see him but is really glad that he is out of town. Meanwhile the young man celebrates his liking for beer – 'its live, white lather, its brass-bright depths' – and briefly considers amorous adventures with the 'plump and plain' middle-aged barmaid.

Ben Evans and the Three Lamps were utterly destroyed in 1941. The *Ben Evans* site became Castle Gardens which, in turn, has become today's Castle Square. On the square there is a cascade featuring a leaf of stained glass designed by the local artist Amber Hiscott. The quotation on the fountain –

We sail a boat upon the path,
Paddle with leaves
Down an ecstatic line of light

– is from 'Rain cuts the place we tread', the unpublished notebook poem written when Thomas was sixteen, in which he describes childhood games in Cwmdonkin Park.

The Three Lamps, more or less on the original site, was rebuilt as a modern pub and part of the *David Evans* department store building, before the *David Evans* complex was demolished. The pub was renamed The Office.

From Castle Street across Castle Square and Princess Way is a view of St Mary's Church. The building was gutted during the blitz of 1941, though by that date successive rebuildings had left little of the original medieval foundation. The present church was rebuilt in 1954–9. The Welsh Guards Falklands memorial, two stained-glass windows, by Rodney Bender, installed in 1985, takes as its theme the Thomas poem, 'And death shall have no dominion'. At the close of 'Old Garbo', a hungover Thomas is troubled by St Mary's ringing bells.

Present-day Castle Street ends at the junction with College Street. The extent of wartime devastation on the Castle Square side of the street is all too evident from Thomas's list of bombed shops and offices in Castle Street and adjoining Temple Street: *Price's Fifty Shilling, Crouch the Jeweller, Potter Gilmore Gowns, Evans Jeweller, Master's Outfitters, Style and Mantle, Lennard's Boots, True Form*, Kardomah, *R. E. Jones, Dean's Tailor, David Evans, Gregory Confectioners, Bovega, Burton's*, and Lloyds Bank.

KARDOMAH CAFÉ

For Thomas fans this is by far the most important of the lost buildings. By a strange quirk of fate the cafe had once been Castle Street Congregational Chapel, where Dylan Thomas's parents were married in 1903. More than three decades later it was the favourite haunt of their son and his friends, who usually sat in what was once the chapel gallery. This was Thomas's 'Home Sweet Homah', celebrated in 'Return Journey' when the narrator recalls the lost voices of 'poets, painters, and musicians in their beginnings'. These included Charles Fisher, who also worked for the local paper and was a published poet, John Prichard, who published poetry and, later, a novel, the painters Alfred Janes and Mervyn Levy, the composer Daniel Jones, and Tom Warner, musician and schoolteacher. Wynford Vaughan-Thomas, later famous as a war correspondent and travel writer, and the poet, Vernon Watkins, made occasional appearances. The group represented a flowering of creative energy unique in Wales. Its talented and opinionated members discussed everything – 'Einstein . . . [to] T. S. Eliot, and girls' – while drinking endless coffees. Something of the atmosphere of those Kardomah days is caught in 'Old Garbo', the place thinly disguised as the Café Royal. Conveniently opposite were the offices of the *South Wales Evening Post*. Thomas's short and unsuccessful career as a junior reporter – its humdrum routine and opportunities for drinking – is also described in 'Return Journey' and fictionalized in 'Old Garbo'. The *Evening Post* kept its eye on its former employee as he rose to fame and reviewed each volume of Thomas's poetry, at times perceptively, and occasionally with absolute bewilderment.

Also destroyed was Lovell's Café. Here, early in the summer term of 1931, the Grammar School Dramatic Society held a 'social' and D. M. Thomas presented the headmaster, D. J. Davies, with a writing case 'in appreciation of the great amount of work he has put into the last three productions of the Society'.

Castle Street ends at the junction with College Street. The latter also had its quota of 'remembered, invisible shops', most listed faithfully in 'Return Journey': *Langley's, Castle Cigar Co., T. B. Brown's, Pullar's, Aubrey Jeremiah, Goddard Jones, Richards, Hornes, Marles, Pleasance and Harper, Star Supply*, and *Sidney Heath*, plus the Wesley Chapel.

High Street, which begins where College Street crosses into Welcome Lane that leads to the Strand, is now a run-down thoroughfare of cheap shops, discount supermarkets and pubs. In Thomas's day its shops and clanging trams made it, as they say in contemporary adspeak, a premier shopping location for Swansea and west Wales. 'Just Like Little Dogs' informs us that even the billiards saloon radiated superiority in insisting that its clients wore collars and ties. Once again, in 'Return Journey', Thomas lists some of the bombed shops and pubs: *Eddershaw's, Curry's, Donegal Clothing Company, Doctor Scholl's, Burton's, W. H. Smith, Boots, Leslie's Stores, Upson's Shoes, Prince of Wales, Tucker's Fish, Stead & Simpson*, plus *Hodges the Clothiers.* On the corner of High Street and Welcome Lane was *Woolworth's*, where Lou, in 'One Warm Saturday', bought the white rose she wore in her hair. The cafeteria waitresses, Thomas recalled in a letter, were often taken out.

Halfway up High Street, on the right, is the Bush Hotel, once residential. Thomas sometimes stayed here when living away and visiting the town. In October 1953, on his last day in Swansea, he drank here with Daniel Jones and others before catching a train for his fatal journey via London to New York. Opposite is The King's Arms, sufficiently near (via an alleyway) to the BBC studios for Thomas to have a 'quick one', or two, or three, before broadcasting. Rabaiotti's Café, where girls could be found, was at No. 33. Near the railway station was long-demolished High Street Arcade, where Snell's had a 'music store' and where Thomas the young reporter often killed time. Nearby was the Mackworth Hotel with its wrought-iron balcony, where 'Return Journey' begins. Opposite is the Elysium Building, once a cinema where the Mackworth barmaid had seen a film, and The Old Red Cow

Inn, echoed in the Red Cow pub in Thomas's screenplay of R. L. Stevenson's story, *The Beach of Falesá.*

Though parts of High Street were badly bombed, on the right-hand side particularly, walking towards the station, above the modern and often tawdry shop-fronts old Swansea facades still survive. But Thomas's High Street can only be imagined. For him or, at least, for his fictive self, it could be a place of intense, urban romantic possibility. In 'Old Garbo' he refers to his 'dead youth in the vanished High Street nights'.

High Street Railway Station still survives, though no longer the Great Western Railway Station Thomas knew. The original concourse, refurbished, was reopened in August 1984 by Wynford Vaughan-Thomas, Dylan's friend and trustee. In 2012 the station was again refurbished and improved. Here Thomas caught the train to London, three hours away, for 'promiscuity, booze, coloured shirts, too much talk, too little work'.

High Street extends past the station. Opposite the station entrance, amid much desolate demolition now turned mainly into car parks, is Ebenezer Street where Ebenezer Baptist Chapel is still to be found. The romantic amnesiac of 'Just Like Little Dogs' walks alone after midnight through 'the damp streets by ghostly Ebenezer'. Parallel to Ebenezer Street is Tontine Street, where Thomas the journalist once covered a chimney fire, or said he did. Lou, that epitome of sexual promise in 'One Warm Saturday', had a 'sing-song Tontine voice', far from refined and thus placing the street as down-market working class.

Even further up High Street, at the end of Prince of Wales Road, is the building that was once Bethesda Welsh Baptist Chapel. Built in 1831, at a cost of £1,600, and rebuilt around 1870, when a florid baroque porch was added, this striking chapel held 1,000 people, and served a congregation that included many of Swansea's *crachach.* The chapel was empty for years, its graveyard overgrown, the building itself falling into ruin. In 'Memories of Christmas' young Thomas is terrified by a story of boys lost in the snow near Bethesda. In general, the building is used by Thomas as an indication of size: Mrs Dacey, in *Adventures*, seems such a pillar of the church that her head could support Bethesda; in 'Quite Early One Morning', in the exotic dreams of sleeping townsfolk, 'Eunuchs struck gongs the size of Bethesda Chapel', this last perhaps an unexpected association for Welsh Baptists. Thomas the young journalist remembered reporting one of its bazaars. Today the building is the headquarters of Swansea's NSPCC and has been extensively renovated.

The car park near the station was once a row of small businesses that included, at 60 Alexander Road, 'Ralph the Books', Ralph Wishart's famous second-hand bookshop, with a newsagent's stall in front. Ralph was a generous friend of Thomas, and kind to all, the present writer included, who loved books and browsed in his shop. For Thomas he was always willing to cash cheques that were more rubbery than substantial. At the very least the car park should have been named after him. The business moved to Dillwyn Street not long before Ralph's death, after which it survived for a few years before closing.

Orchard Street becomes New Orchard Street across the junction with Alexandra Road, and then Dyfatty Street. Up the hill towards Dyfatty traffic lights and behind the high stone wall on the left was the Slaughterhouse. Young Thomas and his friends used to wander past, we are told in 'Reminiscences of Childhood', 'whistling and being rude to strangers'. In 'Where Tawe Flows' Mr Roberts, who worked and smoked in the Slaughterhouse, remembers a caretaker who could break the neck of any rat found in the 'guts-box'.

Alexandra Road continues past Orchard Street. On the right is the Glynn Vivian Art Gallery. The original building, designed by Glendinning Moxham and built between 1909 and 1911, is one of Swansea's finest, with an elegant galleried interior. It was named for the founder, Richard Glynn Vivian, once of Sketty Hall, who gave money and paintings. It has a major collection of ceramics, including much Swansea china. The permanent art collection includes Augustus John's portrait of Caitlin Thomas, Thomas's close friend Alfred Janes's portraits of Thomas, Vernon Watkins and Daniel Jones, as well as paintings by Ceri Richards, Swansea's most famous artist, on Dylan Thomas themes. A shop sells reproductions, mainly postcard size. Next door to the gallery extension and now part of Swansea Metropolitan University is the BBC's Swansea studio, from which Thomas often broadcast. Opposite was Swansea Central Library with its valuable Dylan Thomas Collection. The library has been relocated to West Glamorgan civic centre.

Alexandra Road becomes Grove Place and then De La Beche Street (this last not to be confused with De La Beche Road, Sketty (see page 41)), another manifestation of the Frenchifying geologist. Here begins Mount Pleasant hill.

On the right is the Mount Pleasant Campus of what is now the main part of Swansea Metropolitan University. Part of this site was once Swansea Grammar School. From 1895 to 1910 it was converted into the Swansea Intermediate and Technical School for Boys before separating into two schools – grammar and technical. The wrought-iron 'Technical School' sign over the lower entrance to the present campus from Mount Pleasant Hill survives from that time, and marks the best-placed entrance for viewing what is left of the grammar school buildings.

Founded in 1682 by Hugh Gore, an Irish bishop, after various addresses and vicissitudes the grammar school occupied new Victorian gothic buildings on Mount Pleasant in 1853. Thereafter it flourished. In 1925, when Thomas entered the first form, his

The school on Mount Pleasant hill: Swansea Grammar School in 1935, when D. J. Thomas was still Senior English Master. Dylan Thomas had left in 1931.

father was senior English master and the school had some four hundred pupils. The school motto – 'Virtue and Good Literature' – inspired young Dylan only in part. The uniform was a blazer and a tassled, plush cap of a startling scarlet. The legend that, despite a father known as a martinet in the classroom (his nick-name was 'Le soldat'), Thomas did no work and passed no examinations – 'thirty-third in trigonometry' is what he said – except for English may have been true. More probably there was a gradual loss of interest in things academic as he moved up the school. His unruliness and a school regime liberal in its day are summed up in an anecdote that all must hope is not apocryphal. Caught hiding in playground bushes by the headmaster, young Dylan admitted he was about to play truant. 'Don't let your father catch you', was the head's reply.

The school was badly bombed during the Second World War after which it was relocated to De La Beche Road in Sketty as Bishop Gore Grammar School, becoming a comprehensive school in 1970. Thomas recalls his schooldays in 'Return Journey', citing as highlights not only his editorship of the school magazine but also his success in a spitting championship. A moving sequence describes the bombed buildings, in which 'the names are havoc'd from the Hall and the carved initials burned from the broken wood', and remembers the 'honoured dead'. Today the ruins – essentially of one part of the old complex – have been restored as part of the Metropolitan University. A small Dylan Thomas exhibition can be viewed on request. Behind the Institution are Milton Terrace, Watkin Street and Fuller's Row, whose snow-covered roofs can be seen from bombed and cleared High Street at the beginning of 'Return Journey'.

GRAMMAR SCHOOL TO 5 CWMDONKIN DRIVE VIA TERRACE ROAD

From September 1925 to the summer of 1931, schoolboy Thomas walked this route at the beginning and end of each school day. To return home from school he first walked up Mount Pleasant Hill. On his right, at the first corner, for the first four years of his school life, was Tawe Lodge, Swansea's workhouse from 1861 to 1929. This was, Thomas told Pamela Hansford Johnson, only partially tongue-in-cheek, a feature of his home town. Slightly further up the hill, opposite the church, is the Mountain Dew Inn, where D. J. Thomas and his only friend on the grammar school staff, the Classics master W. S. ('Soapy') Davies, went for quick lunchtime pints. Alcohol did not, it seems, soften D.J.'s robust classroom manner during afternoon lessons. After pub and church, Terrace Road is the main left turn, continuing to the top of Cwmdonkin Drive. In 'Memories of Christmas', Thomas and his friends discuss how they would react to a hippopotamus appearing in Terrace Road; walking from and to school was, however, always more prosaic. In 'Return Journey', Hetty Harris, the lower-class girl chatted up by young Thomas on the Promenade, jeers at him for being still at school; she had seen him on Terrace Road 'with your little satchel and wearing your red cap'. The school cap when new, to judge from the example in the Dylan Thomas Centre's permanent collection, was probably visible to passing ships.

GRAMMAR SCHOOL TO 5 CWMDONKIN DRIVE VIA WALTER ROAD

After turning right at the bottom of Mount Pleasant Hill and walking through De La Beche Street and Mansel Street, the visitor begins 'long, treed' Walter Road, still a fine broad boulevard. Thomas, incorrectly, either apostrophizes it as Walter's or pluralizes it as Walters'. Towards the Uplands, the houses are larger, a reminder that the road was once part of an affluent, middle-class area. Today almost the whole of Walter Road is offices, pubs and restaurants.

At the corner of Walter Road and Humphrey Street is Brunel Court, a modern block of flats. This occupies the site of the demolished Walter Road Congregational Church where a very young Thomas attended the Sunday school, taken there by his mother. In 'Return Journey', 'Walters [*sic*] Road Sunday School Outing' is one of reporter Thomas's journalistic assignments, though this could possibly refer to the Memorial Baptist Chapel at the junction with Burman Street (also demolished before incorporation within a block of flats named Tŷ Sivertson).

The right turn into Humphrey Street leads, first, to Hanover Street, most of which runs parallel to Walter Road. Here lived Mrs Pussie Edwards, whose supposedly dubious morals are mentioned briefly in the classroom scene of 'The Fight'. Humphrey Street leads to precipitous and still-cobbled Constitution Hill, much steeper even than 5 Cwmdonkin Drive, and up which a tramway was once constructed to link with Terrace Road. Near the top of the hill is Rosehill Terrace, where Daniel Jones, then married and with a family, once lived at No. 22. Thomas visited frequently and, when he lived in Laugharne, Jones's home became a refuge from marital quarrels and threatened break-up. In October 1953, during his last visit to Swansea before the fatal journey to New York, he and Caitlin spent some days with Daniel Jones at Rosehill Terrace and in the pubs of central Swansea. There, too, in 1954, with Thomas dead, a drunken and disturbed Caitlin wrecked a room, made crude advances to a visitor and attacked Jones's wife.

Immediately before St James's Church, at the entrance to St James's Crescent, was St Winifride's Convent School for girls, one of whom, black-stockinged and giggly, is the subject of young Thomas's demure fantasies in 'The Peaches'. The convent closed down to be replaced by a private school called Ffynone House. Almost opposite, towards the Uplands, was the High School (later Llwyn-y-Bryn), once Swansea's premier grammar school for girls. Sister Nancy went here, which perhaps explains the moment in *Adventures in the Skin Trade* when Samuel Bennet destroys his sister's school photograph. In that book Walter Road becomes 'Stanley Road'.

Schoolboy Thomas sometimes walked home this way: in 'The Fight', his black-eyed fictional self and bloody-nosed Dan Jenkyn swagger home up Walter Road following the fisticuffs that begin their friendship. Thomas is called 'One eye' by another boy; his good eye sees clouds 'sailing, beyond insult, above Terrace Road'. In a letter of 1939 Thomas recalls his friend, the painter Alfred Janes, then in his still-life period, 'expressing down Walters [*sic*] road with his head full of fruit and stars'.

As Walter Road becomes Uplands Crescent, Eaton Crescent, where Vernon Watkins lived when a boy, is on the left. So is Bryn-y-Môr Crescent. The Phillips family lived at No. 12. Thomas was friendly with the daughters, Evelyn and Vera. Vera married William Killick who in 1945, drunk and suspicious, machine-gunned Majoda, the Thomases' New Quay home.

Gwen James lived at No. 23. She was the elocution teacher to whom young Thomas was sent by his father for the lessons that helped to mould the magnificent voice with the mannered edge that led a few to call him 'Lord Cut-glass'. On the right Mirador Crescent begins, which passes Thomas's dame-school to take the valiant walker into the heart of Cwmdonkin.

DE LA BECHE STREET TO THE BAY VIEW HOTEL VIA ST HELEN'S ROAD

In 'Return Journey' Thomas leaves the grammar school for the town centre by means of De La Beche Street and Gower Street. The latter's 'buildings melted' in the 1941 blitz and after the war it became part of the Kingsway. Opposite the Kingsway's junction with Christina Street was the huge and ornate Plaza Cinema, where the young journalist in 'Old Garbo' shows his press card to get in free to watch a romantic Hollywood film. On Sunday, 1 July 1934, Sir Oswald Mosley brought his blackshirts to Swansea and addressed a fascist rally in the Plaza. Thomas and his friend Bert Trick were part of a communist-led demonstration that ended in scuffles which involved neither. Notwithstanding, Thomas boasted to Pamela Hansford Johnson that he was 'thrown down the stairs' by fascist louts and, as a result, was about to join the Communist Party. The Plaza was demolished and the site redeveloped as a small cinema over a night club and supermarket. The cinema is now itself a night club. The Kingsway ends at the Dillwyn roundabout where 'Ralph the Books' second-hand bookshop struggled on, at least for a while, without Ralph and his glittering literary friends.

Halfway down the Kingsway is Union Street. Near its Oxford Street corner is a health-food shop with a mock-Tudor frontage and lamp still inscribed 'Ye Olde Wine Shoppe No. 10'. This was once the 'No. 10' pub, one of Thomas's haunts, the first-floor bar dominated by a huge stuffed bear. Further down

Oxford Street, next door to Waterstone's bookshop, which is housed stylishly in what was once the Carlton Cinema building, was the Empire Theatre. The site is now occupied by discount clothing shops. In 1931, accompanied by Wynford Vaughan-Thomas, Dylan Thomas, sixteen at the time, interviewed the famous and aged music-hall star Nellie Wallace in her Empire dressing-room. She gave them their first glasses of gin with, as Vaughan-Thomas recalled, 'devastating effect', before finishing the bottle and prancing on to the stage. 'We'll keep this for our memoirs', Dylan told his friend. Thomas heard opera there before the war but, in general, his fictionalized memories of the old Empire were less refined. In 'Old Garbo', young Thomas kills time by scanning the Empire posters for a risqué performance of 'Nuit de Paris' and lusts after the chorus girls: 'Lola de Kenway, Babs Courcey, Ramona Day would be with me all my life'. The names belied, or perhaps suggested, their behaviour: 'I've seen over twenty chorines from the Empire . . . drunk as printers', says the barman in 'One Warm Saturday'.

To the left of Oxford Street's junction with Dillwyn Street and on the corner of Western Street is the Singleton Hotel. During the 1930s it was kept by a Mrs Giles; reporter Thomas, we learn in 'Return Journey', sometimes called in for a lunchtime 'pint and pasty'.

St Helen's Road begins at the red-brick building of Swansea YMCA. From 1929 through 1931 Thomas acted in its Llewellyn Hall with the grammar school's dramatic society and the YMCA Players. He became a pillar of the former, appearing in Galsworthy's *Strife*, and John Drinkwater's *Abraham Lincoln* and *Oliver Cromwell.* In the first he played the lead, in the last the title role. The school magazine reported that 'he looked as young and as fresh and clean as if he had just come off the cover of a chocolate box', which might seem unlike the Cromwell of historical remembrance. The YMCA Players performed mainly thrillers and farces. Llewellyn Hall was not an ideal venue: it was below the gymnasium, which meant that drama was sometimes punctuated by thuds and bumps.

> 'Long St Helen's Road', as Thomas put it, eventually passes a right turning into St Helen's Avenue. In the jumbled topography of 'The Followers' this, it seems, is where its strange heroine Hermione lives, at No. 13, the misnamed 'Beach View'. Leslie and his friend stare through her living-room window. In the same story St Helen's Crescent, in front of the Guildhall, is disguised as a misty 'St Augustus Crescent' through which the young men walk before parting at the old entrance to Victoria Park that is now the Guildhall's front steps.

Towards the end of St Helen's Road is Rodney Street, second left after the Law Courts: the narrator of 'Just Like Little Dogs' thinks the young man spending his evening in the Trafalgar Arch should have 'kids to bounce in a kitchen in Rodney Street'. After the Rodney Street turning, St Helen's Road ends at the main road around the Bay. Suddenly we are in 'One Warm Saturday', one of Thomas's finest stories.

The Dylan Thomas Centre to Mumbles

To walk from the Dylan Thomas Centre in Somerset Place through Adelaide Street is to pass the present *South Wales Evening Post* building. Ahead, in Cambrian Place, is the Queen's Hotel, once a notorious pub where 'shilling women' plied their trade. Nearby is Swansea Museum, 'the museum that should have been in a museum', as Thomas comments in 'Reminiscences of Childhood'. Founded in 1835 as the Swansea Philosophical and

Literary Society, renamed the Royal Institution of South Wales in 1838, with Queen Victoria as a patron, this was the toffs' exclusive answer to the rise of popular libraries. During the 1930s the museum steps seemingly catered for the overspill from the Queen's Hotel: we learn in 'Just Like Little Dogs' that this was where loose and cheap women could be found. Mrs Franklin, in 'One Warm Saturday', illustrates the point, having been seen 'with a black man last Wednesday, round by the museum'.

Oystermouth Road begins to the left of Cambrian Place. On the left was Victoria Railway Station, from which the LMS line ran halfway round Swansea Bay before turning inland. That has long gone, replaced, as has been noted, by a leisure centre. To the right, behind the prison, was the Vetch Field, once home of Swansea City Association Football Club ('Swansea Town' in Thomas's day, and always 'the Swans'). The club has now moved to the ultra-modern Liberty Stadium in Morfa. Though in 'The Fight' Thomas discusses football prospects with new friend, Daniel Jenkyn, in 'Return Journey' he mocks his ignorant younger self for believing soccer results depended on scoring tries.

Oystermouth Road is full of ghosts. But 'the useless railway covered with sand' has disappeared, as has that once famous, tram-like, Mumbles train that ran around the whole bay. In front of the guesthouses, the last arch before the Trafalgar Pub is the Trafalgar Arch, leading to the sands, and over which the railway used to run. This arch is the setting for the whole of 'Just Like Little Dogs': the narrator listens to Tom and Walter discussing their unhappy marriages as they gaze across the bay. The Promenade Man in 'Return Journey' recalls that a much younger Thomas also used to dawdle here.

The area bordered by West Way near the Quadrant, St Helen's Road, and Oystermouth Road, plus the area that is now County Hall, was once the Sandfields. The poet, Harri Webb (1920–94) grew up near here, in Catherine Street near what, in Webb's and Thomas's day, was a poor area. Here, as the latter wrote in 'Memories of Christmas', were the 'desolate poor sea-facing streets' in which gloveless, red-fingered children played in the snow and shouted at Thomas and his well-heeled friends. In Thomas's middle-class Cwmdonkin such children, sometimes thinly disguised, were used as salutary examples: in 'The Fight', for example, having returned home with his black eye he is admonished for being 'as bad as a boy from the Sandbanks'. 'Sandfield boys', he notes rather enviously in 'Reminiscences of Childhood', 'beachcombed, idled, and paddled', seemingly all and every day.

Oystermouth Road ends at the junction with St Helen's Road. On the corner is what Thomas knew as the Bay View Hotel. In pre-war days the sands opposite, on the sea side of tram-lines and the railway, formed the popular pleasure beach known as 'the Slip', complete with beach huts and vendors. Here, on the marine edge of Thomas's 'sea-town', we are seized by his fiction.

'One Warm Saturday', the brilliant short story that closes *Portrait of the Artist as a Young Dog*, begins here. The lonely, romantic poet-narrator wanders across the crowded beach observing family groups, taking part in beach cricket, and listening to soap-box evangelists. He walks unhappily into nearby Victoria Park, 'Victoria Gardens' in the story, and snarls at the flower-clock. Sitting by the 'white-tiled urinal' is a girl who is, as he puts it, 'a bit of God help us all right'. He is too shy to speak to her. Later, in the '"Victoria" saloon', the fictionalized Bay View Hotel, he meets her again and joins her and her friends. Her name is Lou and, although the young man regards her as a romantic ideal, in reality she and her female friends are certainly 'common' and may be prostitutes. At the end of a tipsy evening they all drive from the 'Victoria' to Lou's flat in what appears to be the St Thomas area. There sexual anticipation is utterly disappointed.

The Bay View Hotel, Mumbles train and Swansea Bay at 'the Slip', the setting for much of 'One Warm Saturday'.

The Bay View Hotel is a presence in 'Just Like Little Dogs'. The narrator, eavesdropping in cold Trafalgar Arch, wishes he was in the Bay View's public bar, which had 'a fire and skittles and a swarthy, sensuous girl with different coloured eyes'. Victoria Park, which before the building of the Guildhall in 1932–6 extended as far as St Helen's Crescent, enters three stories through references to its Patti Pavilion, at one time a popular venue for concerts and dances. This was formerly the winter garden at Craig-y-Nos Castle in the upper Swansea Valley where Adelina Patti (1843–1919), the famous soprano, once lived in splendour. She presented it to the town. In each story, Thomas renames it the 'Melba Pavilion', which would hardly have pleased the egotistic and temperamental diva. The grammar school class in 'The Fight' dreams of owning a huge house with a luxurious lavatory as big as the Melba Pavilion. Walter, in 'Just Like Little Dogs', refers mysteriously to goings-on in the ladies' cloakroom during a concert: 'You had to drag the tenors away like ferrets.' In 'Old Garbo', Leslie suggests going to 'a hop at the Patti'.

Oystermouth Road becomes Mumbles Road for the rest of its journey around Thomas's 'bent and Devon-facing seashore'.

The sands, stretching from the docks to Mumbles, are a frequent presence in the writings. In 'Reminiscences of Childhood' young Thomas imagines flying over them. August bank holiday and its crowded beach are celebrated, at length and joyfully, in 'Holiday Memory' and, as has been seen, in 'One Warm Saturday'. They are walked even in winter and even in snow: in 'A Child's Christmas in Wales', Thomas and his friends are 'snow-blind travellers lost on the north hills'. Young Thomas, we learn in 'Return Journey', would 'holler at the old sea . . . [and] mooch about the dunes'. This last may not have been altogether innocent, particularly for a precociously curious boy: the dunes in the middle of the bay's arc were (and remain), at least in summer, a place for amorous adventures. As Mrs Franklin puts it, all too knowingly, in 'One Warm Saturday': 'If you go for a constitutional after stop-tap along the sands you might as well be in Sodom and Gomorrah'. In 'Old Garbo', young Thomas imagines amorous adventures on the sands with barmaids from the Three Lamps and the Carlton. At times, the sands and the bay evoke the cadences of sadness: at twilight, the narrator of 'Just Like Little Dogs' would stare at 'miles of sands, long and dirty in the early dark'. In 'The Followers', the two young men hear 'a ship hoot like a fog-ditched owl in the bay'. The sounds of boats, ships, and foghorns echo through the writings.

Dylan Thomas had little interest in rugby, but he loved cricket and watched it at the county ground at St Helen's. His father sometimes took him to watch Glamorgan there and he played scratch cricket with his friends on the 'bald and cindery surface' of the adjoining recreation ground. Every summer, then as now, the travelling showmen came here to provide 'all the fun of the fair in the hot, bubbling night'. Fairs, wrote Thomas in 'Holiday Memory', were 'no good in the day' but at night the pre-war fair was magical, with its coconut shies, walls of death, Shetland ponies, 'Largest Rat on Earth', 'Most Intelligent Fleas', boxing-booths and ghost trains. But behind the bright lights he sensed a very different world. Hence 'After the Fair', the short story he first drafted in 1933, in which a strange girl with her baby is befriended by the Fat Man.

Opposite the recreation ground, between Mumbles Road and the sands, are the Cenotaph and Promenade, the latter now mainly used by joggers, dog-walkers and cyclists. During the 1930s, this was the place for what south Wales valleys folk called a 'monkey parade'. Young people walked out after Sunday evening church or chapel, the young men whistling after the girls, intending to meet each other and perhaps pair off. From the Promenade the beckoning dunes were only a few steps away. In the more modest 1930s this last may well have been, for the well-brought-up, more a theoretical than a practical advantage. In 'Return Journey', the Promenade is where eager young Thomas is mocked by Hetty Harris's friend not only for having being seen in school uniform, but also as 'Mr Cheeky, with your cut-glass accent and your father's trilby'. Then he triumphs, comparatively speaking, over female prevarication.

At the junction of Mumbles Road and Brynmill Lane is the main southern entrance to Singleton Park. In Thomas's boyhood Vivian's Stream, once the boundary of Swansea Borough, not only ran to the sea parallel with the Brynmill wall of the park, as it does today, but also flowed under Mumbles Road and on to the beach near the Brynmill Arch. Thomas, as a young boy, used to play in the water, says the Promenade Man in 'Return Journey', 'dawdle in the arches . . . and lark about on the railway-lines'.

> Also in 'Return Journey', the narrator leaves Mumbles Road via Brynmill Terrace (now the lower part of Brynmill Lane) en route for Uplands and Cwmdonkin Park.

After Brynmill Arch and Singleton Park, Mumbles Road passes Swansea University. Here, Daniel Jones pursued a brilliant student career in the Department of English, before turning to music. Thomas, who later came to regret neglecting his studies, always avoided academics. He had good reason to avoid Kingsley Amis, who lectured in that same Department of English for ten years from 1949, knew Thomas, and heartily disliked him and his work. But, long before Amis, Thomas doubtless visited his friend on what was then a very small campus and, oddly, coupled the university with London as two 'very big and bewildering places'.

OYSTERMOUTH AND MUMBLES

At Blackpill the dunes give way to a sea-wall and walkway which continues into 'beery and fleshly' Oystermouth.

The shopping arcade halfway up Newton Road was once the Regal Cinema. Fictionalized Thomas the journalist, whose press-pass facilitated cinema-going, saw *White Lies* here, featuring the actress Connie Bennett in a foam bath and, in 'Old Garbo', reports as much to his coffee-drinking pals in the Café Royal. 'Too much foam for me, old man', replies his friend Leslie. Newton Road becomes New Well Lane, continuing up the hill to Newton itself, where Daniel Jones lived during his last years, drinking regularly at the Newton Inn. Here is Paraclete Congregational Chapel. One of Thomas's maternal aunts ('Auntie Dosie') was married to the minister, Reverend David Rees, whom she had met when he was minister at Canaan Chapel in St Thomas. As a small boy, Thomas sometimes stayed with them in the nearby Manse and attended the Sunday school. David Rees retired in November 1932 and Thomas, about to bow out as a journalist, wrote a piece in the *Herald of Wales* entitled 'End of a Great Ministry': 'Mumbles, and indeed the whole of Gower, will lose one of its best-known and best-loved inhabitants'. In reality, he hated his uncle, and is said to have written in a letter: 'I hate you from your dandruff to your corns'. David Rees, as 'The Reverend Crap, a pious fraud' and 'The Reverend Crap, a holy pimp', is the subject of 'Matthias spat upon the lord', the notebook poem, unsurprisingly unpublished, of 16 August 1933. He thought the boy was mad.

Mumbles is another area full of ghosts. At Southend, Swansea Little Theatre was based in the small church hall during the 1930s. From 1932 to 1934 Thomas acted here in a wide range of plays, from *Hay Fever* to *The Beaux' Stratagem* and *The Way of the World.* All ended in predictable fashion: he liked to slip out of rehearsals for a quick drink, and did so once too often for the producer's liking. At a dress rehearsal she issued an ultimatum which Thomas ignored and so left the company, leaving it to manage as best it could.

The quick drinks were usually consumed at the Marine Hotel, subsequently known as Vincent's. This pub is now The Village Inn. Two other Mumbles pubs have strong Thomas associations. One is the Antelope Hotel, on the corner of Mumbles Road and Village Lane, opposite the putting course, also convenient, then, for the Little Theatre. It is not always open. The Mermaid Hotel, however, with its stylish frontage and wrought-iron balcony, plus extensive Thomas connections, was demolished following a fire. The rebuilding turned it into flats for young people plus a restaurant, which has since closed. Thomas would have been appalled, its bar, 'the womb of the Mermaid', was dear to his heart. Even at seventeen he was a regular: 'Muse or Mermaid?' he asked himself in a letter, with prophetic indecision. When in Ireland he wrote wistfully of his 'Mumbles Mermaid (bless her hair and her tail)'. In the early skit, 'Spajma and Salnady', Salnady creeps up the stairs of the Mermaid for what was then, before pubs opened on the Sabbath, an illegal Sunday drink with the manageress. In 'Return Journey', which, alas, does not go as far as Mumbles, we learn that Thomas broke his front tooth in the Mermaid when playing a game called 'Cats and Dogs'. After a few (or more than a few) drinks, to amuse his friends he pretended to be a dog, scampering about on all fours and barking, before running out to the nearest lamp-post which he bit, breaking the tooth. In September 1934, when he imagined himself in love with Pamela Hansford Johnson and hoped to marry her, she and her mother visited Swansea to meet the family. They stayed at the Mermaid. The visit was a disaster: it rained every day, the Johnsons discovered Thomas was younger than Pamela had believed, and she had hysterics.

Thomas loved Mumbles, though sometimes he regretted the effect of 'the oystered beer'. Because of the family connection up the hill in Newton, Mumbles was, for Thomas, 'where the aunties grew'. 'Fourth Drowned . . . Alfred Pomeroy Jones', in *Under Milk Wood*, was born there. The pier was 'gaunt . . . with . . . skeleton legs'. Standing beneath it at low tide, we learn in 'Just Like Little Dogs', was 'no good in the rain'. None the less, unhappily married Tom '"spends every Sunday under the pier," the pug-faced young man says bitterly. "I got to take him his dinner in a piece of paper."' Beyond the pier, out to sea, are the two islands that probably gave the place its odd name (a corruption of '*Mamelles*', from the French, meaning breasts, which is presumably what Thomas had in mind when he told Pamela Hansford Johnson that Mumbles was 'a rather nice village, despite its name'). On the outer one is the Mumbles lighthouse, the beams from which are seen by the cold young men in 'Just Like Little Dogs', who stand aimlessly in the Trafalgar Arch. The same lighthouse is, in 'Old Garbo', capable of the ultimate distraction: couples in the lascivious dunes 'lay loving under their coats and looking at the Mumbles lighthouse'. Since 1793 there have been various structures on that rocky outcrop, as the second highest tide-fall in the world rushes past. Mumbles lighthouse marks the outermost seaward edge of the city.

2

Gower – 'the loveliest sea-coast'

Dylan Thomas's Gower – an introduction

For Dylan Thomas, Gower was a crucial place, a formative influence. He knew it before the rise of the car and mass tourism. During schoolboy summers he camped there or visited with his friends. In the period between leaving his job as a local journalist in 1932 and moving to London two years later he spent many hours on 'one of the loveliest sea-coast stretches in the whole of Britain'. He wrote this in a letter of early December 1933 to Pamela Hansford Johnson, adding that he often spent whole days on a peninsula much of which, he considered, had been little affected by modern times. A month later, in January 1934, he told the same correspondent that he spent afternoons 'walking alone over the very desolate Gower cliffs, communing with the cold and the quietness'. Sometimes he walked with friends, stopping at convenient pubs. Mostly, it was, as he said, a place to 'commune'. No one can remember him bathing in the sea – though he did so on at least one occasion – but he was once photographed daring to paddle, wearing his trousers rolled.

Since Thomas's death this tiny area – only eighteen miles long, three at its narrowest, eight at its widest – became the first to be designated, in 1956, an Area of Outstanding Natural Beauty. It now includes three National Nature Reserves, Sites of Special

Scientific Interest, and much Heritage Coast owned by the National Trust. The villages are no longer untouched by time. They have been discovered by incomers and second-homers, and the popular bays have car parks and caravans. That said, sensible planning controls and the combined efforts of many, including the local authority, the Gower Society and the communities themselves, have ensured that Gower has not been spoilt. Were Thomas to return he would still find what attracted him: the magnificent coastline with fine sandy beaches, Norman castles and churches, and monuments even more ancient. In winter, at least, it can still provide opportunities to commune.

Thomas's friend, Bert Trick, the 'communist grocer', had a holiday bungalow on Gower, and it was there, in 1932, that Thomas talked of writing a Welsh *Ulysses*, the germ of what, many years later, became *Under Milk Wood*. An event of a very different kind occurred two years later: at Whitsun 1934 he had, or said he had, a wild and drunken threesome with a friend and a girl with a 'loose red mouth'. Thomas 'confessed' to Pamela Hansford Johnson, then his girlfriend with whom he had recently stayed in London, that he had spent three drunken nights with the girl in a bungalow on Gower. Biographers remain sceptical of Thomas's claims, suspecting a plot to cool the relationship with Pamela. She forgave him, but the decline and eventual fall of the relationship can probably be dated from this event.

That association did not alter his affection for the peninsula. During the Second World War he was appalled at the idea of Gower being bombed. Swansea, of course, had been bombed regularly through the summer of 1940 before the devastating blitz of the following year. Thomas and Caitlin were staying in Wiltshire; his mother reported that Gower had become a refuge from the raids, with Swansea folk sleeping on the beaches, in barns and under hedges. 'Bury your poems in a stout box', he advised Vernon Watkins, who was still at home in Pennard.

Dylan Thomas and Gower's literary history

Gower's unofficial laureate is Vernon Watkins (1906–67), who lived at Pennard for much of his life and wrote many poems on Gower themes. These include 'Bishopston Stream', 'Rhossili' ('Spindle of the moon! Turning-place of winds, end of Earth, and of Gower!'), and 'Hunt's Bay', as well as 'Taliesin in Gower', 'Taliesin at Pwlldu' and a number of Gower ballads. He was not the first nor the last to find inspiration on the peninsula. In medieval times, Lewys Glyn Cothi (*c.*1420–89) and Dafydd y Coed (*fl.* late fourteenth century) both celebrated generous patrons in what was then the Lordship of Gower and Kilvey. More recent writers include famous figures. In 1794, Walter Savage Landor (1775–1864), one of Dylan Thomas's 'Poets of Swansea', wrote 'Voyage to St Ives, Cornwall from Port-Einon, Glamorgan':

How gladsome yet how calm are ye
White birds that dip into the sea!
How sportive those bright fins below
Which through green alga-meadows glow!

How soft the lustrous air around,
And the red sail's is all the sound,
While me my heart's fierce tempest drives
On from Port-Einon to St Ives.

'This is the cleanest coast I ever saw', considered Francis Kilvert (1840–79) in 1872. David Jones (1895–1974) writes in *The Sleeping Lord* of the Stone Age skeleton once called the 'Red Lady of Paviland' but now known to be male, found, as Jones puts it, in the 'carboniferous vaultings of Gŵyr'. Harri Webb (1920–94), John Ormond (1923–90), Dannie Abse (b.1923), J. C. Evans (b.1923), Sally Roberts Jones (b.1935), the American William Virgil Davis (b.1940), Catrin Collier (b.1948), and Stephen Knight (b.1960), are among others drawn to Gower subjects. The true heir to Vernon Watkins is perhaps Nigel Jenkins (1949–2014), born in Gower, who explores his rural upbringing, Gower scenes, and much else.

Apart from his own writings, Dylan Thomas contributed to the literary history of Gower the final article in his series on 'The Poets of Swansea'. His subject is E. Howard Harris (1876–1961), 'the first poet of Gower'. The titles of Harris's volumes speak for themselves. They include: *An Exile's Lute* (1919), *The Harp of Hiraeth* (1922), *Songs in Shot Silk* (1924) and *Singing Seas* (1926), which suggest he was brought up in the romantic middle ages. Thomas praises his ambition, his intense response to Gower's beauty and romance, but attacks his execution: 'He starts well, gains in intensity, and falls in a single phrase, to the murkiest depths of bathos'. He advised Harris to spend more time on his writing in order to eliminate the hackneyed. Thomas was seventeen when he wrote the article; Harris was a 56-year-old schoolmaster, and not a modest man. His reaction was predictable.

Dylan Thomas's Gower

KILLAY TO VENNAWAY LANE

For Raymond Price and young Dylan Thomas, in 'Who Do You Wish Was With Us?', the next place on their walk from Uplands through Sketty en route for Rhosili would have been Killay. On their right, in the suburb's centre, as they follow the A4118, is The Black Boy Inn. In these politically correct times the old inn-sign of an eighteenth-century young black servant has been replaced by a nineteenth-century collier-boy. We can surmise that Thomas once drank here, if only because he drank in most Swansea pubs. Certainly he knew of it: in 'The Londoner', Thomas's radio drama of 1946 about a day in the life of a London family (in some ways a trial run for *Under Milk Wood*), the local is called the 'Black Boy'. In that time of post-war shortages, it is a pub that frequently runs out of beer.

The main road continues up the steep hill through Upper Killay, whose folk, wrote E. A. Dillwyn in *The Rebecca Rioter: A Story of Killay Life* (1880), were 'a rather rough set'. Upper Killay is now a trim suburb on a busy main road where Swansea meets Gower at Fairwood Common. The fictional friends in 'Who Do You Wish Was With Us?' cross 'the spreading heathered common . . . in the heat mist wasting for miles on either side'. The hill and the heat destroy pedestrianistic ambition: guiltily but eagerly they flag down and board the bus to Rhosili. Once across the common on the South Gower road, immediately before Kilvrough Manor that bus would have passed the turning into Vennaway Lane (B4436).

LANGLAND TO VENNAWAY LANE

Thomas's coastal Gower begins at Langland Bay. He sometimes walked there with friends from the Little Theatre group, threatening to go 'rude bathing' but never even taking off his socks. The parents of friends of his had a beach hut which he visited. He probably took Pamela Hansford Johnson there when she and her mother came to Swansea, assuming the rain stopped long enough for them to get off the bus. In the next bay, Caswell, they were photographed arm in arm and embracing. In one snap, Thomas is demonstrating the lost art of kissing his girlfriend with a cigarette still in his mouth.

The B4593, Caswell Road, leads up the hill from the bay to Pyle Road in Bishopston. This last is an old Gower village much enlarged since the Second World War, though even in 1939 Thomas described it as 'a crowded piece of beautiful landscape'. After turning left into Pyle Road, Pyle Corner is the first sharp bend.

On the left is the road to 'comfortable, wild' Pwll-du Bay, where Bishopston Valley meets the sea. Thomas had difficulty pronouncing the name, or so he said to girlfriend Pamela. During the nineteenth century limestone was

The ultimate in active and passive smoking: Pamela Hansford Johnson and Dylan Thomas at Caswell Bay in 1934.

quarried at Pwll-du, a legacy of which is the huge pebble bank at the back of the bay. The quarrying also explains why the two private houses – 'Beaufort House' and 'Ship House' – behind the huge pebble-bank, were once pubs. During 1934 Thomas had lunch outside what was then the Beaufort Arms and reported to Pamela, on what was presumably a day short of newsworthy events, that he had seen a rat.

At Pyle Corner, Pyle Road becomes Bishopston Road. When Thomas's parents moved here from Cwmdonkin in 1937, they lived at 'Marston', 133 Bishopston Road, almost halfway between Pyle Corner and the Joiner's Arms, which Thomas used as his local when he came to stay. Marston (the name can no longer be seen) is a semi-detached, bay-windowed house similar to 5 Cwmdonkin Drive, but much smaller. Dylan, Caitlin and infant Llewelyn, impecunious and homeless, spent the Christmas of 1939 here. They also returned during 1940, fleeing from their creditors in Laugharne and from the hostility of those who, unlike Thomas, had not managed to evade military service. Vernon Watkins had not yet been conscripted and he often walked with the Thomases along Pennard cliffs and through beautiful Bishopston Valley. The family was again at Marston in 1941, for almost four months. They were, Thomas reported to John Davenport, 'cooped up here, in little boiling rooms, quite broke'. Pipes burst in a January frost. Inevitably relations were strained, particularly between Caitlin and Florence Thomas, and particularly when through the latter's suspicions Thomas learned of Caitlin's relationship with the musician William Glock. A violent row followed, during which Thomas threw a fork at his wife. This was a turning point in their marriage.

In 1941 American troops were stationed in the Bishopston area and manoeuvres took place near the sea. 'Girls hot and stupid for soldiers flock knickerless on the cliff', Thomas wrote in a letter. In his opinion, Bishopston had become 'God's least favourite place'.

D.J. would certainly have agreed. During 1941 the intensified bombing of nearby Swansea forced Thomas's parents into rural Carmarthenshire and a cottage at Blaen-cwm owned by D.J. They never returned.

Bishopston Road continues until its junction with Pennard Road (B4436). This last continues left through Kittle, ceasing to be the B4436 at the right-hand junction with Vennaway Lane. At this junction is Pennard Church, with a memorial plaque commemorating the fact that Vernon Watkins sometimes worshipped there.

Pennard Road continues through Southgate village to the National Trust car park on Pennard Cliffs. To the right of the car park, at the beginning of the cliff path that leads, eventually, to Pobbles Bay, is Heatherslade. Now an old people's home, much altered and extended, this was Vernon Watkins's family home during the 1930s. From 1935 Thomas was a frequent visitor; the friends discussed poetry, read to one another and walked the cliffs and beaches. Watkins loved sea-bathing and on at least one occasion persuaded his friend to join him. This was the first time that he had ever bathed, Thomas said, and a long time since he had taken so much exercise. He had become 'your hearty, Britain-chested, cliff-striding companion'. Such activities were not addictive. At Heatherslade they played croquet, and post-supper card games such as lexicon. Sometimes Thomas brought his friends, Alfred Janes being one. In due course Caitlin came with her husband and joined in the croquet. Ghosts, 'the things of light', flit, even now, across the geriatric lawns.

Next door was 'Windyridge' where Watkins's friend, Wyn Lewis, lived. Lewis was the same age as Thomas and, by a strange coincidence, had once played in Cwmdonkin Park, scuffling with Thomas's friends. When Caitlin was

Dylan and Caitlin Thomas in 1937.

present Thomas was always suspicious of good-looking Wyn.

Even further along the West Cliff path is 'The Garth'. After their marriage in 1944 Gwen and Vernon Watkins eventually settled here to bring up their children. To this small, prefabricated bungalow – 'chalet-like', said Philip Larkin – Thomas and his Swansea friends were frequent visitors. They discussed literature or simply fooled around. At 'The Garth', one evening in November 1940, Thomas completed 'Deaths and Entrances', his poem about the London blitz that *Horizon* published in 1941 and which became the title poem of his finest volume. Gwen Watkins had great reservations about Thomas the man, and even more about his lifestyle. She could hardly forget that Thomas had failed to turn up when best man at their London wedding. At her Pennard home she caught glimpses of a different, more attractive Dylan, modest about his work, lying on the grass discussing Dickens or, in the twilight, playing the children's game 'Statues' with her husband and Daniel Jones.

VENNAWAY LANE TO RHOSILI

Vennaway Lane connects with the A4118, the South Gower Road that crosses Fairwood Common. This road leads to Parkmill, up the hill to Penmaen, and on to Nicholaston. Alfred Janes once lived and painted here, in Nicholaston House, to the north-west of Nicholaston Church.

> To the right of the road is Cefn Bryn, in English 'ridge hill'. This is the high spine of the peninsula, running for four miles down its centre. Cefn Bryn offers spectacular views north and south, and 'Arthur's Stone', the remains of a prehistoric chamber tomb with a capstone weighing about twenty-five tons. During the early 1930s, after the Little Theatre had performed a play in Gower, Thomas led nervous members of the cast on a night walk over an eerie, seemingly ghostly Cefn Bryn.

Across the fields from the South Gower Road are the beautiful bays from Three Cliffs round Oxwich Point to Port Eynon. The two friends in 'Who Do You Wish Was With Us?', still on their way to Rhosili on that sunny summer's day, note 'the ash-white of the road, the common heathers, the green and blue of fields and fragmentary sea'. 'Down there is Oxwich, but you can't see it', says Raymond Price, before they take the bus.

The A4118 continues, after Oxwich, round the dog-leg at Llanddewi and on to Port Eynon with its Landor connection. This was not a Thomas place. To reach that it is necessary to follow the bus carrying Raymond Price and young Thomas. At Scurlage it turns right off the A4118 into the B4247, the road to Rhosili.

Before Rhosili the road passes the turning to Mewslade. In the *Portrait* story 'Extraordinary Little Cough', young Thomas and his school friends camp during the August holidays in a field on the cliffs between the two places. For some, this is not for the first time: they feed their friends' anticipation with tall tales of midnight dances and of 'elderly girls from the training college who sun-bathed naked'. Immediately after arrival they walk down a 'wooded valley' before flinging themselves down on the sands of Mewslade beach. In the standard biography Paul Ferris points out that much of 'Extraordinary Little Cough' demonstrates the fine line – perhaps, at times, the absence of any apparent line – between fiction and real life in Thomas's short fiction. Many details were taken from the life: the gramophone playing popular songs of the time, the older girls staying nearby. Brazell and Skully, the school bullies who camp nearby and terrorize the younger boys, actually existed. Ferris draws on the memories of John Bennett, one of Thomas's camping friends, who recalled that food and money sometimes ran short, the boys made daily – and presumably increasingly desperate – visits to the post office hoping for a postal order from home and, in recollection at least, always had good weather.

RHOSILI

Rhosili has spectacular cliffs, sands and views, and a dramatic, serpent-like promontory known as Worm's Head. At the far end of the bay's arc, hidden by Rhosili Downs, is the village of Llangennith, a surfers' paradise 'very near nowhere', which Thomas sometimes reached on what he described as his 'medicinal walks'. When the whole scene is viewed from the cliffs it is easy to understand why Vernon Watkins wrote such an ecstatic poem, and why the place has attracted enough writers – Sally Roberts Jones, John Powell Ward and Catrin Collier among them – to fill a small car park that, in high summer, would have to be reserved.

In the middle of the arc is an isolated house that was once Rhosili Rectory. In 1948, when the Thomases lived in squalor in the Oxfordshire village of South Leigh, they were desperate to return to Wales. 'I wish I were in Rhossili', he wrote to Vernon Watkins, and this longing may well have influenced Margaret Taylor, the most generous of Thomas's patrons. At this time and again in 1953, when problems occurred regarding the ownership of the 'Boat House', she considered buying the rectory for the family. Thomas's earlier view of Rhosili as 'the wildest, bleakest, and barrennest [bay] I know', and of the worm as 'the very promontory of depression', may have played some part in the idea falling through. A more practical reason was that before the development of the Worm's Head Hotel the village had no pub. Even if a pub had existed in Rhosili village, visiting it from the rectory would have meant a long and dangerous walk back on a dark night for someone who liked a drink or four. The 'Boat House' was always a more attractive proposition.

In 'Extraordinary Little Cough' George Hooper, the 'Little Cough' of the title, runs the length of Rhosili's magnificent sands, over three miles in all, to prove to the mocking boys that he can do it. Thomas himself, as a fine schoolboy runner, achieved this feat more than once. The Dylan Thomas enthusiast can then step out of one short story into another. Or rather, back into another: for Raymond Price and young Thomas, in 'Who Do You Wish Was With Us?', this was journey's end. They stare at the 'very long golden beach' before walking the cliffs and the causeway to the very end of the Worm's Head: 'shading my eyes like Raleigh in some picture . . . [I bellowed against the wind] "Why don't we live here always? Always and always. Build a bloody house and live like bloody kings!"' They stay too long on the Worm and get cut off by the tide. There the story leaves them, with hours to wait until the tide recedes.

Dylan Thomas once suffered the same fate. He kept warm, wrote Vernon Watkins, by running and clapping his hands. On another occasion Thomas, with Caitlin, Vernon Watkins, and

Wyn Lewis, had to rush across the Causeway as the tide flowed in. An unfit Thomas lagged behind and had to be pulled from the water by Watkins. 'You nearly caught us napping on the Worm', Thomas later wrote to his friend. When he stood at the end of the Worm and gazed due west Dylan Thomas may or may not have known that the contours of the world dictate that the next landfall is what, for him, was North America's fatal shore. Those who believe in premonitions may well find significance in the fact that Dylan Thomas, his small staring figure overwhelmed by the scenery, was drawn so frequently to the very end of Gower.

3

Laugharne – 'this timeless, mild, beguiling island'

Dylan Thomas's Laugharne – a brief history

'. . . WALKED FROM ST. CLEAR to Larn (or Laugern) . . .' wrote Coleridge in his notebook on 17 November 1802. The entry reminds us that Laugharne's literary history did not begin with Dylan Thomas, and that the name has always caused problems.

As the bilingual road signs inform all who visit the town, Laugharne (pronounced 'Larn', as Coleridge knew) is derived from the Welsh Talacharn. But though 'tâl' means 'the end of', the meaning of 'acharn' is obscure, though some argue that it refers to the headland above the River Coran or Corran. An earlier form of 'Corran' may have been 'Corram'; certainly in the twelfth and thirteenth centuries, some documents refer to Laugharne as 'Abercorram' ('the mouth of the Corram'), as distinct from the more generally used 'Abercorran'. To complicate matters further, the name 'Laugharne' is derived from 'Lacharn', itself an abbreviation of 'Castell Talacharn'. The problems of the name are a philologist's nightmare, or perhaps delight.

The original settlement may have been prehistoric and possibly Roman. Its importance is explained by its site, at the mouth of the River Taf, overlooking its estuary. It is also at the confluence of the Taf and the much smaller river Coran, the latter being little more than a brook, which flows between upper and lower Laugharne before entering the estuary. When the Normans came in the late eleventh and early twelfth centuries, overland travel would have been difficult because of the state of the roads, in winter at times almost impossible. The shortest and quickest routes from south-east to west Wales were either by sea or by a series of fords or ferries from peninsula to peninsula. Thus the Normans built their castles – including those at Kidwelly, Llansteffan and Laugharne – to guard the river entrances and estuaries. Laugharne Castle protected the ferry from the Llansteffan peninsula – it landed at a point slightly further up the river from the 'Boat House' – and the estuary from marine marauders.

Laugharne is an ancient borough. Its charter dates back to the reign of Edward I (1272–1307) and was given to the town by Sir Gwydo de Brione, the younger son of a powerful Norman Marcher lord. It still has a mayor called a portreeve, who wears a chain of golden cockleshells, a corporation called a grand jury, which still meets every two weeks to deal with the business of the town, and an ancient burgess roll. Meetings are held in the small Town Hall in King Street; beating the bounds takes place on the Whit-Monday of every third year.

Merlin is said to have prophesied that

> Kidwelly was;
> Carmarthen is;
> But LAUGHARNE shall be
> The greatest city of the three.

Though such a statement has not furthered Merlin's reputation for long-term prescience, during parts of the Middle Ages it may not have seemed unreasonable. Henry II came to Laugharne Castle in 1171–2 to negotiate a peace with Rhys ap Gruffudd, ruler of Deheubarth and opponent of Norman authority in south-west Wales, but it was a peace that lasted only until the king's death in 1189. In 1415 the town sent archers to Agincourt. During the sixteenth century Sir John Perrott (1528–1592), then a favourite of Queen Elizabeth I, owned the castle as well as that at Carew in Pembrokeshire, and he set about converting both into grand Tudor mansions. Perrott gave his name to Sir John's Hill to the south of the town and, in due course, to one of Dylan Thomas's finest poems. But he lost favour at court, was convicted of high treason and died in the Tower while awaiting execution.

In 1644, during the Civil War, the castle was besieged by Parliamentarian troops commanded by Major-General Rowland Laugharne. A bombardment from cannon stationed on Glan-y-Môr, the hill above what is now Dylan's Walk, and then on the prophetically named Fern Hill on the other side of the town, caused much damage. The Royalist garrison eventually surrendered. Parts of the castle were later demolished so that it could no longer be used as a stronghold. The end of the siege also marked the end of Laugharne's importance as a military, political or administrative centre.

Laugharne had a not undeserved reputation, gained mainly in the sixteenth and seventeenth centuries, as the haunt of pirates and wreckers. By the early years of the nineteenth century, however, it had mouldered into a very different kind of place. In 1803 it was visited by Benjamin Heath Malkin, an English teacher who travelled through Wales before publishing his important travel book, *The Scenery, Antiquities and Biography of Wales* during the following year. Malkin wrote:

> The descent to Laugharne is highly romantic . . . It is one of the most sequestered places that can be conceived; and is much inhabited by half-pay officers, and families which seek an economical retirement. It is by far the best built little town in Caermarthenshire, and very well supplied with provisions; but its heat in summer is intolerably oppressive.

The 'Boat House' and Sir John's Hill: a house fit for a poet and a hill that inspired one of Thomas's finest poems.

It is almost as if Laugharne was the setting for *Persuasion*. A year later E. Donovan, who, like Malkin, was averse to snappy titles, published *Descriptive Excursions through South Wales and Monmouthshire in the Year 1805*:

> Laugharne is a neat, compact, seaport town, of small importance: in a situation the most retired imaginable, and is therefore seldom visited by strangers. It lies in no direct road to any place of consequence, neither are the accommodations, I have reason to suspect, inviting . . . although the place is literally crowded with petty alehouses, not one of several at which we enquired, could furnish even a mug of ale. When malt is dear they abstain from brewing in this place.

This was hardly a Laugharne that would have attracted Dylan Thomas.

The town is, of course, the product of its past. Even today, traces of its Norman heritage linger in placenames: 'The Lacques', for instance, in wet lower Laugharne, or the hamlets of Delacorse to the north of the town. Laugharne is an 'Englishry'; English, to quote Sir John Edward Lloyd, 'is the native tongue'. In his *A History of Carmarthenshire* (1935) Lloyd suggested that the language was introduced along the coastline by Teutonic invaders in the twelfth century. The strong Norman presence doubtless also played a part. What is certain is that Laugharne has remained an English-speaking and 'Church' enclave within Welsh-speaking and chapel-going Carmarthenshire. From his Welsh-language standpoint Aneirin Talfan Davies considered, in 1955, that Laugharne's 'Englishness . . . [is] as if it is rooted in the soil, and this is what gives one the feeling of being in a foreign and strange country'.

Laugharne was once a port, but the quay and warehouses on the Green Banks near the castle car park had disappeared long before Dylan Thomas's first visit to the town. A few small boats left on the mud by the tide are all that remains of Laugharne's maritime heritage. It has never been a market town. The railway never came. Nor did industry. As late as the 1920s the River Taf yielded rare pearls from mussels. These last are now extinct, as are the Taf coracles. In Thomas's day, there were still cockles in the estuary and a cockle factory on The Strand for boiling and shelling the molluscs before they were taken to Carmarthen market and elsewhere. The cockle beds are fished out; the factory is now an apartment block.

When Dylan Thomas came to Laugharne it was – and to some extent still is – an isolated, atmospheric, somewhat down at heel, and rather eccentric place. The home of pirates and wreckers remained prone to lawlessness. The upper and lower parts of the town, known as 'Up Street' and 'Down Street', were fierce rivals; Constantine Fitzgibbon compared the inhabitants of both, too glamorously, to Capulets and Montagues. The town had a reputation for violence, usually fuelled by drink, which included fighting with knives. The high insanity rate of pre-war Laugharne hardly contributed to calm. Certainly eccentrics abounded: the ferry man was deaf and dumb and doubled as the town barber, and one inhabitant always dressed as a Wild West cowboy. Town events could descend into chaos as the committee drank the time away.

Malkin's half-pay officers had long gone. Laugharne in the 1930s was a predominantly working-class community with much unemployment, and its main income was the dole. The few educated, middle-class residents included the clergyman and the writer Richard Hughes. The town's doctor lived five miles away in St Clear's. Laugharne, wrote Constantine Fitzgibbon, 'fitted Dylan like a single, eccentric, tattered glove'.

Laugharne's literary history

Turner painted a famous view of Laugharne Castle, Morland Lewis the Strand. There have been many attempts at the 'Boat House', one of the most recent being Gordon Stewart's. But it must be said that Laugharne's literary history is more important. It has always attracted writers. One early visitor was Jeremy Taylor (1613–67), chaplain to Charles I and, after the Restoration, bishop of Down and Connor and then of Dromore. His *Holy Living* (1650) and *Holy Dying* (1651) place him in the front rank of writers of English prose. Taylor's second wife was a Carmarthenshire heiress, and he had connections with Golden Grove near Llandeilo. As chaplain to the Royalist forces in west Wales during the Civil War he may well have been in Laugharne when the castle was besieged. According to tradition the brass candlesticks sometimes used on the high altar in St Martin's Church were presented by him.

A later and even more famous connection is with Mary Wollstonecraft (1759–97), wife of William Godwin and herself the author of such important feminist works as *Thoughts on the Education of Daughters* (1787) and *A Vindication of the Rights of Woman* (1792). Her father bought a farm near Laugharne where the family lived for periods between 1776 and 1782. Her daughter became Mary Shelley (1797–1851), the author of *Frankenstein* (1818) and wife of the famous Romantic poet. Legend has it that Mary Shelley herself once stayed at 'Great House', at the point where Clifton Street becomes King Street, though, if this did occur, it would have been long after the Wollstonecrafts had left the district.

The ubiquitous Walter Savage Landor was a visitor. During the 1790s when he lived in Tenby and, as has been seen, in Swansea, he became friendly with Howell Price, a Carmarthenshire gentleman who lived in Laugharne. Price's step-daughter was Rose Aylmer, to whom Landor addressed his most famous poem. But though he had pleasant times with Price and the Aylmers, 'Written at Larne', his poem published in 1806, tells a different story. It laments the malevolent fate that drove him from Ipsley Court, one of the Landor family homes in Warwickshire, to a very different part of the world:

> Here never Love hath fann'd his purple flame,
> And fear and anger start at Freedom's name.
> Still, high exploits the churlish nation boasts
> Against the Norman and the Roman hosts.
> 'Tis false! – where conquest had but reapt disgrace
> Contemptuous Valor spurn'd the reptile race.
> Let me once more my native land regain . . .

From which we conclude that Landor did not much like the ordinary people of 'Larne' or, indeed, with exceptions, the Welsh. He once described the latter as 'creatures . . . somewhat between me and the animals . . . as useful to the landscape as masses of weed or stranded boats'.

Coleridge, in his diary entry for 17 November 1802, described in detail his visit to Laugharne, beginning with his

> first view of Larn with its fine richly ivied Castle close upon the sea, & its *white & all white* Houses, interesting – unfortunately at low Tide – or I should have seen the Castle washed by the sea – The Bay is a great river of Greenish Water taking one bend among fieldy hills . . . Mallows – Furze – Lychens/Cottage with its dunghill of Cockle shells . . .
>
> A number of handsome *glassy* Houses in Larn/never saw such a profusion of tall broad Windows, except in Hamburg . . .

> Cottages favorable only to vegetable Life . . . the shrivelled Shrimps of cold & Hunger – swarthied Tenants/
>
> White Church with grey Steeple a furlong or so from the Town . . .

Coleridge spent some time in the churchyard recording tombstone inscriptions, mainly of the very young and the very old. He commented:

> While I took the copy, the Groundsel showered its white Beard on me/ Groundsel & Fern on the grave, & the Thorns growing that had been bound over it –
>
> On a square Tomb as high as half up my Thigh, where the Tom Tits With their black velvet Caps showered down the lovely yew-berries on me. Here lyeth the Body . . .

He then, it seems, returned to St Clear's.

More than a century later Edward Thomas (1878–1917), the poet and prose-writer who was killed on the Western Front, and who is now regarded as a leading writer of the period, stayed at Mrs Wilkins's boarding-house in Victoria Street from 1 November until 17 December 1911. This was a period of his life during which he was at times much depressed, occasionally almost suicidal. He wrote from Laugharne to a friend: 'Sometimes I feel wellish here, sometimes very bad; never well, I never can be well again without a miracle'. None the less, he kept busy. While at Laugharne he completed his study of George Borrow, corrected proofs of *The Icknield Way* and began work on a book on Swinburne. The work helped him control his depression, and he was able to write some cheerful letters to his wife Helen. In 1913 he published *The Happy-Go-Lucky Morgans*, his only published novel. This contrasts 'Abercorran House' in Balham, South London which is demolished to make way for Abercorran Street, with an instantly recognizable Abercorran: 'Abercorran town itself, the long grey and white street, with a castle at one end, low down by the river mouth, and an old church high up at the other'. The contrast is between a haunted, mythical, certainly idealized landscape, part of Edward Thomas's romanticized Wales, and the urban life of Welsh exiles in a London suburb. In April 1914, before war put an end to such pleasures, he returned to Laugharne as part of a cycling holiday with his two children and stayed for an enjoyable week. It seems no accident that Dylan Thomas was drawn to his namesake's poetry. In 1949 he devoted a broadcast to him in which he read a number of Edward Thomas's poems. These included 'The Child on the Cliffs' which is set in either Gower or Laugharne.

The novelist Hilda Vaughan (1892–1985) often stayed in Laugharne in a holiday home bought by her father. Her husband, Charles Morgan (1894–1958), in his day a famous novelist, sometimes accompanied her. He stayed with Richard Hughes in August 1939, and Dylan Thomas reported to John Davenport that 'we're going along tonight to be dazzled'. To judge from 'Quite Early One Morning', in which he writes that even dreaming of reading Charles Morgan was like being woven 'into a refined and precise grey comma', he was not. Hilda Vaughan's *Harvest Home* (Gollancz, 1936), a story of innocence threatened by violence, is set in the south-west Wales port of 'Abercoran' in 1800. Vaughan draws on Laugharne's association with wreckers, and uses some topographical details: the 'Great House', the Church with its yew trees set 'on an eminence outside the town', the salt-flats and the clogging, sucking sand of the estuary. To earn a few pence the heroine, Eiluned, joins the cockle-pickers far out on the 'moist sand and grey slime' of the cockle beds.

Richard Hughes (1900–76) lived in 'Castle House' from 1934 through the Second World War (spent mainly in London, working for the Admiralty) until 1946. As the successful author of *A High Wind in Jamaica* (1929) and a number of plays, and having married a wealthy wife, the painter Frances Bazley, Hughes lived in some style as the de facto squire, involving himself in the life of the town. In time he became petty-constable of Laugharne. This was a post very much in keeping with the town's eccentricity:

duties were mainly honorary, and the symbol of office was an old chair-leg with a piece of string tied to it. While at 'Castle House' Hughes wrote a volume of children's stories – *Don't Blame Me!* (1940) – and, more importantly, the Conradian *In Hazard* (1938), his second novel, in which the loss of a ship in a storm can be linked to events leading to the Second World War. Much of his writing was done in the gazebo on the castle's seaward wall. In 1946 the family moved from Laugharne to Talsarnau in Merionethshire where Hughes wrote the first two novels (of a projected four) of *The Human Predicament*, his epic but unfinished novel-sequence centred on the Second World War. Volume one, the much-praised *The Fox in the Attic* (1961), begins with a fine description of sea-marshes that owes much to those near Laugharne. 'The tiny, unique self-governing township of Flemton', where parts of the early chapters are set, draws some details from the place that, for twelve years, had been Richard Hughes's home.

Other writers of note have strong connections with Laugharne. One is Lynette Roberts (1909–95), author of *Poems* (1944) and *Gods With Stainless Ears* (1951). Both volumes were published by Faber on T. S. Eliot's recommendation. She lived for some years in Llan-y-bri, only a few miles from Laugharne on the Llansteffan peninsula across the estuary. After separating from her husband, Keidrych Rhys, the famous editor, she moved to Laugharne in 1949 with her two children, Angharad and Prydein, and lived in a caravan. The preface to her volume of 1951 is dated from 'The Caravan, Laugharne. 15th November 1949'.

Gods With Stainless Ears is about a wartime relationship between a Welsh village girl and a gunner on active service. It opens with coastal scenes –

> Saline mud
> Siltering, wet with marshpinks, fresh as lime stud

– familiar to all who know the estuarial mudflats around Llansteffan and Laugharne. More poignant are lines from her

Laugharne period that suggest her caravan was parked near St Martin's Church:

> Sitting surrounded by wasps,
> My only view in this lovely
> And sad caravan
> Are the graves and tombs filling
> Each window pane
> Clustering up the sweet earth.

The second is Kingsley Amis (1922–95). He had little time for either Thomas or his writings, even though his friendship with Stuart Thomas, the Swansea solicitor who dominated the Dylan Thomas Trust, led to him becoming a trustee. Amis was strangely drawn to Laugharne, and he wrote much of his Booker prize-winning novel, *The Old Devils* (1986), in 'Cliff House' on the hill above the 'Boat House'. In part 7 of this novel the protagonists stay at Birdarthur, a village closely associated with the poet Brydan, who is based on Dylan Thomas. The place is similar to Laugharne, having a 'Brydan's Walk', the poet's grave in the churchyard, a favourite bar where visitors congregate, and some crass commercialism (such as 'Brydan's Burger Bar'). Amis's satire is not friendly: his village, formerly a port and site of quarrying and heavy industry, has been revived as an enterprise zone.

The third is Vernon Watkins, of whom more below, who visited Laugharne to visit his friend. He wrote affectionately, in 'A True Picture Restored', of

> that toppling house
> Over the village hearse,
> Where the Portreeve assembled
> His birds and characters[.]

A fourth is Margaret Atwood (b.1939), the distinguished Canadian writer who has family links with Wales. Her short story

'The Grave of the Famous Poet' in *Dancing Girls and Other Stories* (1977) explores an uneasy love-relationship that finally founders during a visit to Laugharne. The couple explore the down-at-heel town in what may well have been the late 1960s or early 1970s – the castle is derelict, the empty 'Boat House' in decline; only the grave is well tended. The story offers a glimpse of Laugharne after Thomas and before the age of CADW and popular tourism.

Dylan Thomas and Laugharne

Dylan Thomas first visited Laugharne with the writer Glyn Jones in May 1934. They both had family on the Llansteffan peninsula and came to Laugharne on the ferry-boat from a point near Black Scar. In a long letter to Pamela Hansford Johnson he duly reported on the town's Englishness and the presence of Richard Hughes. He described at length women gathering cockles in the estuary, noting the grinding physical strain of such work, and looked forward to a drink that evening at the Three Mariners pub. Laugharne was, he considered, 'the strangest town in Wales . . . Today . . . a hell-mouthed mist is blowing over the Laugharne ferry'. Two months later it was 'the nearest approach under the sun to a Stygian borough'.

In 1938 he brought his new wife, Caitlin, to live at 'Eros' in Gosport Street. In a letter to Henry Treece, who wrote the first book-length study of his work, he described Laugharne as a place with 'three good pubs . . . the best bottled mild in England'. Later that same year, having removed to 'Sea View' in 'Up Street' Laugharne, and deeply in debt to most local tradesmen, it was still 'a lovely town' but full of creditors. Eventually, with Caitlin pregnant, they placated some tradesmen and fled to Hampshire to stay with Caitlin's mother. Two months after Llewelyn's birth the family moved back to 'Sea View' where, apart from periods at Bishopston and Blashford, they stayed until July 1940. In August 1939, even the Thomases could not avoid 'this war, trembling even on the edge of Laugharne', even though through the phoney-war period of that September Laugharne was a quiet refuge, 'this

'Eros', 2 Gosport Street, Laugharne today, with a view of 'Boat House'. Newly-married Dylan and Caitlin's first home. It was dingy and waterless. Neither liked it.

cockled city . . . sweet and quiet . . . so slow and prettily sad', as he wrote to Bert Trick. That feeling tended to counter occasional homesickness. Looking forward to a Christmas reunion in Swansea as 1939 ended, even 'the castle and the pretty water make me sick', he admitted to Charles Fisher.

They left in July 1940, partly because Laugharne's tradesmen eventually ran out of patience and served writs for non-payment of bills. In addition, Thomas's successful evasion of military service and tendency to gloat about his manoeuvrings hardly endeared him to those who had to serve. Above all they left because the war had destroyed Thomas's income: *The Map of Love* (1939) was published only a few days before war broke out, *Portrait of the Artist as a Young Dog* (1940) during the Battle of Britain. Both sold hardly a copy. Magazines had closed. Dylan and Caitlin went to Marshfield in Gloucestershire to stay with rich John Davenport. Eight years were to pass before Laugharne saw them again.

In 1948, then living *en famille* in Oxfordshire, for part of the time looking after his ageing parents, Thomas was eager to return to Wales. Margaret Taylor, ever the generous patron and would-be lover, was prepared to buy a property for the family. Laugharne became the most appealing place: 'the best town, the best house, the only castle, the mapped, measured, inhabited, drained, garaged, townhalled, pubbed and churched, shopped, gulled, and estuaried one state of happiness', he rhapsodized. He fancied 'Gosport', the large house up the hill from 'Eros', but the owners would not sell; he thought of 'Castle House', Richard Hughes's old home. Eventually Margaret Taylor purchased the 'Boat House' for £3,000 and the family moved in during spring 1949. It was to be Thomas's home until he died.

During his final years Thomas was not always complimentary about the place to which he was so eager to return. The 'weather gets me like poverty: it blurs and then blinds, creeps chalky and crippling into the bones, shrouds me in wet self, rains away the world', he told Marguerite Caetani, 'Princess Caetani', who lived in sunny Rome and was the wealthy American owner of *Botteghe Oscure*, the famous literary journal which published much of Thomas's later work, including part of *Under Milk Wood*. To Charles Fry, head of Allen Wingate, the publishers to whom Thomas had failed to deliver a commissioned book on America, Laugharne, in early 1953, was 'this wet idyllic tomb on the coast'. A few months later John Malcolm Brinnin, the American responsible for Thomas's reading-tours, was told that Laugharne meant 'torpor and rain and Ivy's dungeon', this last referring to Brown's Hotel, then kept by his close friend Ivy Williams. In each case Thomas wrote in hope of financial gain or the receipt of favours, hence, possibly, his desire to make his life seem as gloomy as possible.

Certainly 'Laugharne', recorded for the BBC and used in a live programme from Laugharne's Memorial Hall on 5 November 1953 – the day on which the news reached Caitlin of her husband's collapse in New York – is a wholehearted tribute in which the town is described with great affection as 'this timeless, beautiful, barmy [both spellings] town . . . a legendary lazy little black-magical bedlam by the sea'. The broadcast demonstrates why Thomas loved the place: the way it stood chaotically back from life's mainstream, so often rejecting such social norms as work, order and respectability. 'Bedlam by the sea' appealed to Thomas; he and Caitlin contributed their fair share. Thomas, of course, also dramatized Laugharne's ever-lurking anarchic spirit in *Under Milk Wood.*

Laugharne and Under Milk Wood

The origins of *Under Milk Wood*, as has been noted, go back to the 1930s when Thomas sat in Bert Trick's Gower bungalow and talked vaguely of writing a Welsh *Ulysses*. Thereafter, with hindsight we can see him preparing through his short life for what became and remains his most popular work. The material was provided by those small seaside places, such as New Quay, Laugharne and Ferryside, in which he lived or which he knew. His work for the BBC taught him broadcasting techniques; such features as 'Quite Early One Morning', 'The Londoner', 'Margate – Past and Present' and 'Return Journey', in particular, can be seen as trial runs for the 'Play for Voices'. His wartime scriptwriting for Strand Films and Gryphon Films taught him accessibility and fostered a concern for immediate response. His marvellous letters, especially those from the 'Boat House' period, dramatize everyday events in the interests of humour and pathos.

As for places: there are always attempts to explore geographical links, both of the predictable and the surprising kind. Mumbles, which, in Thomas's day, had its quota of retired seamen and characters, is sometimes mentioned although, with the exception of general ambience and experience, convincing links are hard to establish. Ferryside in Carmarthenshire, opposite Llansteffan across the Towy estuary, has become another candidate. Certainly, there were family connections between his father's family in Johnstown and relatives of Beryl Hughes of Ferryside, and D. J. Thomas visited the village, as did his son. According to Hughes,

Dylan often left the train to Carmarthen at Ferryside to drink in the local pub and visit her relations, and she claims the originals of Captain Cat and Schooner House are her Uncle Dick and his home at 2 Neptune Villas. Beryl Hughes offers interesting background material, but her 'evidence' is circumstantial, often tenuous, and too often unconvincingly assertive.

Links with New Quay are different in kind. Thomas and his family lived near New Quay from September 1944 to early summer 1945. 'Quite Early One Morning', the short radio feature first broadcast in December 1944, is, as everyone knows, an imaginative description of the place. The feature is based firmly on the town's topography; the final section introduces us to characters whom we meet again in *Under Milk Wood.* Thomas's drawing of Llareggub is also based on New Quay.

Almost certainly the play reflects, consciously or unconsciously, Thomas's experience of all four places. Like most writers he picked up unconsidered trifles wherever they could be found. However, we can be sure of three things. One is that *Under Milk Wood* belongs to the aftermath of the Second World War. When Thomas began seriously to write the play he first called it 'The Town That was Mad': a town is certified as mad and dangerous and so cordoned off from the world by means of barbed wire and sentries 'lest its dotty inhabitants infect the rest of the world', as Thomas put it. The town is found to be sane and, regarding itself as the only sane part of a demented world, wishes to remain apart. Llareggub is a place set aside from the world, even though the play tends to suggest that escaping the world is ultimately impossible. *Under Milk Wood* is a product of the nuclear age and the Cold War, of the time when Thomas was settled in the 'Boat House'. Secondly, of the suggested locations only Laugharne possessed the play's anarchic spirit. Thirdly, Thomas never lived in Mumbles, had only brief links with Ferryside, and after a short stay in New Quay never went there again. Laugharne drew him back, again and again. And though he discovered, all too often, that life eventually caught up with him no matter where he was, he continued to think of Laugharne as an ever-present help in trouble, where, he believed, he could be 'an upright man' in an unjudging and nicely disordered place. And yet, as Gwyn Jones pointed out in an early review of *Under Milk Wood*: the world of the play is 'a quintessence of Laugharne; it is Laugharne lifted above particulars and raised to universals'.

Dylan Thomas's Laugharne

CASTLE CAR PARK TO 'EROS'

All visits to Thomas's Laugharne begin in the car park under the Castle walls in 'Down Street', lower Laugharne. Here is Green Banks with its boats, where the harbour once was. For Thomas it was the 'dwindling harbour', viewed from afar in 'Poem in October'. In 'Over Sir John's Hill' this was at the centre of his

> Crystal harbour vale
> Where the sea cobbles sail[.]

Across the car park from the Castle, on The Strand, is the apartment block that was once the 'cockle factory'. The main road away from the castle is Gosport Street. A hundred or so yards up the hill on the left-hand side and opposite a small car park, is 'Eros', 2 Gosport Street, a former fisherman's cottage which was Caitlin and Dylan Thomas's first home after their marriage. They lived here from May to July 1938, inheriting the name.

'Eros' is now a private house, uPVC'd and with all amenities. The cottage rented by the Thomases was very different. It was full of old furniture which they both hated, as they did the scarlet wallpaper. Nor did they like the cottage itself, described by Thomas as 'pokey and ugly, four rooms like stained boxes'. It was damp and wholly without services and there was only an earth lavatory. Water had to be carried from a pump in The Grist, the square at the bottom of the hill; Thomas was often sighted in his dressing gown, carrying a bucket. But then, they both often shopped in dressing gowns. Thomas rarely bathed; Caitlin, more fastidious, bathed in the sea, which could be reached from the bottom of their garden. Though occasionally sighted in the Corporation Arms, at the bottom of the hill, they were invariably short of money. At times they lived on cockles which they collected themselves, or on the occasional rabbit or fish that 'happened' to come their way. They rolled their own cigarettes, Dylan very inexpertly, Caitlin deftly, publicly and sexily on her thigh. George Tremlett comments that, half a century later, older townsfolk still remember them as 'the first hippies to arrive in West Wales'.

From the rear of the cottage are tremendous views of the estuary, the castle and the 'Boat House'. These, however, did not inspire: during his three months at 'Eros' Thomas completed few poems, a state of affairs that worried him. He began revising 'On no work of words', which became part of *The Map of Love.* It was not completed until after the Thomases had moved to 'Sea View'. In a revision inserted into his notebook and dated 'Laugharne. Sept. 1938', he looked back at a barren summer, much of which was spent at 'Eros', in lines omitted from the published version:

> For three lean months now, no work done
> In summer Laugharne among the cockle boats
> And by the castle with the boatlike birds.

He did, however, finish 'One Warm Saturday', which became the final *Portrait* story, and he reviewed fiction for *New English Weekly.*

CASTLE CAR PARK TO THE 'BOAT HOUSE' VIA WOGAN STREET

Wogan Street leads up the short hill from The Grist, with its 'stunted' war memorial, to 'Up Street' Laugharne. Ahead is 'Castle House' where, as has been noted and as the plaque indicates, Richard Hughes and family once lived and where the

Thomases stayed for some months during 1941. It is a superb Georgian building, perhaps the grandest in the town, with a fine entrance hall and staircase, and a ballroom. When Hughes first occupied it the house was in poor condition, and the architect Clough Williams-Ellis, creator of Portmeirion, was brought in to sort it out. It would become the setting for frequent bohemian house-parties during the 1930s. Augustus John was a frequent visitor and, in 1936, he was accompanied by Caitlin Macnamara, then his model and mistress. Earlier that year Thomas had met her in London and begun an affair with her. Back in Swansea and hearing she was in Laugharne, on 15 July Alfred Janes drove him to visit her. Later that day a drive through west Wales with Caitlin, accompanied by Augustus John, ended with fisticuffs between John and Thomas outside a pub in Carmarthen. Thomas had the worst of it, but the day marked the true beginning of the relationship that led to their marriage the following year.

Behind 'Castle House' is a garden; photographs of Dylan and Caitlin relaxing here, with their children playing on the grass, are now in the great Dylan Thomas collection in Austin, Texas. In Hughes's day the garden included the castle, where his guests could stroll or sit in deck chairs. This was the 'collapsed castle' of Thomas's essay, 'The Crumbs of One Man's Year'; more famously, it was 'the castle / Brown as owls' of 'Poem in October'. The gazebo which, as has been noted, was used by Hughes as a writing-room, was probably built on the base of a medieval tower during the nineteenth century by the then owner, Richard Starke, who also developed the gardens. Through 1938 and 1939, Hughes gave Thomas permission to use the gazebo for his own work. Fortified by bottles of wine stolen from Hughes's fine wine cellar within the castle walls, it was there that Thomas wrote most of the stories that comprised *Portrait of the Artist as a Young Dog* (1940). Once, when Vernon Watkins visited, the two spent a long sunny afternoon in the castle grounds reading Rilke's *Duino Elegies*. During 1941, with Hughes away at the war, Thomas, he told Vernon Watkins, wrote poems in 'the romantic, dirty summerhouse looking over the marsh' and Caitlin danced alone in the empty ballroom. The castle is now controlled by CADW, which has stabilized the ruins and restored Starke's garden, and the public are admitted during the summer months.

First right after 'Castle House' is cobbled Market Lane. Years ago, for obvious reasons, this was called 'Hangman's Lane'. On the corner with the main road is the Town Hall where, through the centuries, the portreeve and grand jury sat (and still sit) fortnightly to deal with the town's business. The building has a meeting room and a small jail. The clock on the tower, wrote Thomas, 'tells the time backwards'. Market Lane leads to 'Sea View', the Thomases' home from July 1938 to July 1940. They rented the property from Ebie and Ivy Williams, so generous to Thomas over the years, who owned Brown's Hotel and much else in Laugharne. 'Sea View' is double-fronted but thin, three storeys high and only one room deep; like a doll's house, thought Augustus John. The name remains on the original gate pillars. It became sadly dilapidated but, under new ownership, has been refurbished. The house is now a small hotel and part of a national chain of similar establishments.

The house was let unfurnished but, as luck would have it, an aunt of Caitlin's died and she inherited her furniture. Vernon Watkins gave them a radio, even though the house lacked electricity. They bought a double bed on hire-purchase, but failed to make the payments of seven shillings a month, had it repossessed and were forced to sleep on the floor on a mattress. They used tea-chests as tables or as a desk. All else they begged or borrowed. Though they went back to Caitlin's mother's home in Hampshire for the birth of their first child, Llewelyn, on 30 January 1939, they returned when he was two months old. He was baptized in St Martin's Church, Laugharne, with Augustus John, Richard Hughes and Vernon Watkins as his godfathers.

Dylan and Caitlin settled into a domestic routine. Caitlin did what was expected of her, that is she kept house and cooked the meals, the latter so often consisting of a stew into which almost

Three generations of the Thomas family. Rear: Dylan Thomas and son Llewelyn. Seated (left to right): Aeronwy, Florence Thomas, Colm and Caitlin. Front: Mably the dog.

anything might be thrown. Her husband gave her little help. Vernon Watkins came to stay more than once and the two friends walked and talked poetry. Watkins once offered to clear the table after a meal. Thomas told him grandly that that was women's work; men's work was to write their poems. Caitlin was initially compliant, but later she was to react very differently. They were always short of money and it was during this time that Thomas concocted the scheme that he called 'Thomas Flotation Ltd': a dozen more affluent writers would contribute five shillings a week to enable him and his family to live. His friend John Davenport organized the appeal but, predictably, it yielded little.

They had many visitors, who often found their way to bed using candles stuck in empty beer bottles. One was the painter Rupert Shephard, whose portrait of Thomas reading in the sitting-room is now in the National Portrait Gallery. Others included old friends from Swansea, Henry Treece, even Augustus John, who stayed the night. Richard Hughes was, of course, only a few yards away; the two families exchanged visits and the Thomases attended Hughes's parties.

As usually happened when Thomas had a comparatively settled existence, he began writing more poems and stories, often, as has been said, in the Castle Gazebo. It was one of the most prolific periods of his maturity. During the 'Sea View' period his poems, new or revised from the notebooks, included 'A saint about to fall', 'If my head hurt a hair's foot', 'The tombstone told when she died', 'Twenty-four years', 'Once it was the colour of saying', 'Because the pleasure bird whistles', 'Unluckily for a death', 'To others than you', 'When I woke' (with its Laugharne setting), 'Once below a time', and 'There was a saviour'.

Years later, Caitlin Thomas recalled Vernon Watkins's belief that the Thomases' two years at 'Sea View' had been 'the happiest period of our lives together. I think he was right.' After the Second World War, Watkins saw the house once more. His wife has written that 'when he saw it again and remembered how happy they had been there in spite of their poverty, he told me he felt ill with sorrow and desolation'. Watkins's poem 'To a Shell', published in the posthumous volume, *Fidelities* (1968), commemorates that moment:

> A house facing the sea.
> Hard and bitterly
> Though waves beat on that wall
> From the swirling quicksands of debt,
> I swear that it cannot fall.

Yet, even at 'Sea View' dark clouds were gathering. During the final months of their occupancy Thomas completed 'Into her lying down head', a troubled poem that appears to be about Caitlin's infidelities and his own sense of exclusion. It preceded their sudden, debt-laden departure from Laugharne. They left behind, and lost, all they possessed. This last not only included their furniture, but also, it seems, the heart of their marriage.

Market Lane joins Victoria Street, where Edward Thomas once stayed. A right turn out of Market Lane leads to what was once Cliff Road but has been renamed Dylan's Walk. This leads past the entrance to 'Cliff House', with its Kingsley Amis connections, eventually to the 'Boat House' itself. First stop, however, is Thomas's 'Work Hut'.

CASTLE CAR PARK TO THE 'BOAT HOUSE' VIA THE FORESHORE

On the Castle side of the car park a small stone bridge crosses the River Corran. The path in front of the castle passes the gazebo on the castle wall in which, as has been said, a wine-filled Thomas wrote most of *Portrait of the Artist as a Young Dog.* Thereafter a stone causeway runs along the foreshore. It is covered at high tide. The causeway ends in an easy climb across rocks and a steep flight of steps. At the top of the steps is the 'Work Hut'.

'WORK HUT' AND THE 'BOAT HOUSE'

The 'Work Hut' was originally a garage, built by a Dr Cowan to house Laugharne's first motor car (a green Wolseley). The Cowans owned the 'Boat House', which they used as a holiday home between 1906 and 1918. Although when Thomas converted the hut into a study it was warmed by a stove, the wooden building proved damp and draughty in the winter. It was certainly hot on sunny summer days: he wrote to Hector MacIver, a Scottish acquaintance, 'My study, atelier, or bard's bothy, roasts on a cliff-top.' It was, he told Princess Caetani in 1952, his 'wordsplashed hut'; in 'Poem on His Birthday', one of his last poems, it is 'the long tongued room . . . his slant, racking house'. It was his 'water and tree room on the cliff'.

Usually he worked there only in the afternoons, for he had settled into the familiar routine: pottering in the morning, perhaps writing a letter or reading, or visiting his parents, whom he had installed in a house in King Street, to do a crossword with his father. After a session in Brown's Hotel and a fatty lunch, usually one of Caitlin's stews, he would work at his poems or, perhaps, one suspects, fall asleep, drowsy with beer on warm summer afternoons. Sometimes he would creep back into Laugharne, where he could be found reading a thriller in his parents' home. Wherever he spent the afternoon Thomas was usually back in the 'Boat House' by 7 p.m. He would have a bath – personal hygiene appears to have improved since his 'Eros' days – during which he ate dolly mixtures or pickled onions before having a meal and returning to the pub.

The interior of the 'Work Hut', which can be viewed through a small glass window, has been restored to resemble the shed when Thomas used it, even down to discarded papers on the floor and a strategically placed though empty bottle of beer. The whole is an interesting example of tourist kitsch. Through the hut's other windows are views of the estuary and of Sir John's Hill. For some years after the reconstruction a board was attached to the shed which, in oddly gothic script, read: 'In this building Dylan Thomas wrote many of his famous works, seeking inspiration from the panoramic view of the estuary.' Protests followed the removal of the notice, which photographs had given international circulation. Carmarthenshire County Council has replaced it with an information stand.

The 'Work Hut' is only a few yards from the steps down to the 'Boat House', which nestles under the cliff. Its origins go back at least to the early nineteenth century. The name probably refers to its early use as a boat-building and repair centre; what is now the yard at the rear was once a dock filled by the tide and which could also be used as a dry dock. Given the building's fairly isolated position it may well have had early links with smuggling.

The house has two storeys on the garden side, three on the rear. The River Taf runs past through its channel in the estuary, disappearing into each incoming tide. At high tide the sea washes against the lower walls, under the verandah, so that the house seems almost to be floating. At night this effect is intensified. It is described vividly by Lorraine Scourfield in her official guide to the house: 'Lights flickering from the farms across the estuary, the cries of sea-birds and lapping waves can create the impression that the Boat House is indeed a steady ship out at sea.' That estuary, Thomas's 'dabbed bay', with its pools, shifting sands and herons, is a major influence on his poetic language.

When the Thomases moved into the 'Boat House' in May 1949 in some ways it must have seemed like a return to 'Eros'. The house hinted at paradox in being both damp and without mains water. Until the ever-generous Margaret Taylor paid for mains connections they were forced to use a nearby well. In Thomas's day the house had six small rooms and a kitchen. He was graphic about the outside toilet: 'There are rats in the lavatory, tittering while you shit', he told John Davenport. Caitlin Thomas, however, showed a domestic side for which she has not received much credit. Despite being pregnant with Colm Garan (Welsh for 'heron'), their second son and third and last child, who was born in Carmarthen hospital on 24 July 1949, she worked hard to make the house homely. In this she was helped by Dolly Long – remembered by Aeronwy Thomas as 'our treasure' – of 49 Orchard Park Estate, the small group of council houses above the town. Dolly was the 'daily' who looked after two-year-old Colm when both Dylan and Caitlin went to America in 1952. The furniture in the 'Boat House', in itself fairly cheap, was brightly painted, coal fires burned in the grates, while photographs, coloured postcards and magazine clippings enlivened the walls. In his bedroom, Llewelyn, the eldest, favoured photographs of African tribesmen. The Thomases' own bedroom was dominated by a large dressing table draped with net and ribbons which was Caitlin's pride and joy. As he moved in he wrote to Margaret Taylor: 'this is *it*: the place, the house, the workroom, the time'. Alas, such initial euphoria did not last. In November 1952 he wrote to Princess Caetani of 'this tumbling house whose every broken pane and wind-whipped-off slate, childscrawled wall, rain-stain, mousehole, knobble and ricket, man-booby-and-rat-trap, I know in my sleep'. Family life degenerated, too swiftly and too often, into fierce often violent marital quarrels and into poverty through fecklessness. The visits to America hardly helped.

Dylan Thomas lived at the 'Boat House' for three-and-a-half years. The period was punctuated by three visits to North America, plus a fourth from which he did not return alive, four months in Camden Town, in another house paid for by Margaret Taylor, and a short visit to Iran in 1951. When away from Laugharne, he tended to drink heavily. Despite steady earnings from the American tours and frequent broadcasts, mainly poetry readings, he was constantly in great financial difficulty. During this settled yet often disturbed and restless time, the long sometimes muzzy afternoons in the 'Work Hut' yielded a small number of essays, short stories and reviews. He wrote, but did not quite finish, *Under Milk Wood.*

He completed only six poems, thus averaging less than two per year. These were 'Over Sir John's Hill', 'In the White Giant's Thigh', 'Poem on His Birthday', 'Do not go gentle into that good night', 'Lament' and 'Prologue'. Two others – 'In Country Heaven' and 'Elegy' – remain unfinished. The poems respond to his father dying and dead, to ideas of death and failing powers, to notions of annihilation linked to contemporary fears of nuclear catastrophe, and to his own predicament. This last is sadly evident in the first part of 'Prologue': the house 'seashaken', the rocks 'breakneck', his writings 'sawn, splay sounds'. There are positives, of course: his love for his father and the latter's dignity in death, the beauty and power of nature, his poems as surviving 'arks'. Two of the poems are among the finest he wrote. 'Over Sir John's Hill' arranges the view through the 'Work Hut' window into a symbolic statement about death in nature and life as precious. 'Do not go gentle' urges his dying father to set aside a disappointing life and be true to himself. Yet, overall, these last poems reflect the clouds gathering daily not only over the estuary but around Thomas himself.

Shortly after Thomas's death in New York on 9 November 1953, Caitlin left for Italy. Dylan Thomas's widowed mother, Florence Thomas, then moved in for five years. By the late 1960s the house once owned by Margaret Taylor was in trust for Caitlin and her children. In 1973 she sold it for £22,500 to Ffynone House School Trust, a private school in Swansea. It planned a Dylan Thomas Memorial and Field Study Centre, repaired the property and opened it to the public in 1975. Maintenance costs eventually forced Ffynone to withdraw and the 'Boat House' was sold to Carmarthenshire County Council for £27,500. An expensive programme of renovation then began.

The building nestles under cliffs. Above these are woods, hence Thomas's description, in 'Prologue', of living 'At a wood's dancing hoof'. The cliffs themselves are of red sandstone and fundamentally unstable. Since the 1930s, when the Cowan family lived there, there have been danger warnings. These were not heeded until, in 1983, the boundary wall collapsed into the front garden, followed by further subsidence, rockfalls and earth slides. In 1989 a successful programme of works was carried out to stabilize the cliff, and to repair the verandah and the sea wall, financed jointly by Carmarthen District Council and the European Regional Development Fund.

The 'Boat House' today has been extensively refurbished, not always successfully. Outside, the rusting, rotting verandah has been renewed, as have some windows and doors. Regrettably, in some ways, the dock at the rear has been filled in and paved. The first floor, where the Thomases had their bedrooms, is now divided into a small video studio and a picture gallery with small displays of Thomas material. This serves tourists but at the expense of some of the atmosphere. Part of the ground floor is a small reception area and shop.

The living room, also on the ground floor, is furnished in the style of the 1930s and 1940s, and well worth the visit. The fireplace with its red surround is as it was in Dylan Thomas's day. Most of the furniture came with Florence Thomas when, after D.J.'s death and that of her son, she moved in for those five years. The desk against the window was originally in D. J. Thomas's study in 5 Cwmdonkin Drive. The two armchairs, plus the stylish sofa, also come from there, as did the winged chair, which was Florence

Thomas's favourite. The low wooden chair was also in Dylan Thomas's boyhood home and was the only chair the visiting washerwoman was allowed to use, a vivid insight into pre-war class attitudes. The crutches were Florence Thomas's, used in her old age. There are photographs of Thomas and family. In one corner is a period radio wired to play Thomas's recorded voice.

We can be sure that the present-day sitting room is much cleaner and smarter than it would have been in Dylan Thomas's day. None the less, the recreation directs a shaft of light into that suburban world in which Thomas grew up and which influenced him so profoundly. The present writer first saw this room in the early 1970s, when house and contents were squalid. On the mantelpiece were books borrowed from Carmarthen Library Service, all with return dates in November 1953, the month Dylan Thomas died. He would smile at that, one would guess, if only at having evaded payment of the sizeable fine. The basement has a small cafe – excellent Welsh-cakes served by a friendly staff – with some tables outside on the paved former dock. This area is sometimes used as a small auditorium.

A few yards to the right from the top of the 'Boat House' steps, Dylan's Walk becomes a path through the trees above the river. Below is the old 'Ferry House', once linked by boat with the Llansteffan side of the estuary. In 1934, when Thomas paid his first visit to Laugharne with Glyn Jones, he landed here. Subsequently he used the ferry to visit his mother's family around Llan-gain and Llan-y-bri. If necessary, the ferryman would carry passengers on his back across the mud, as he did with Thomas on one photographed occasion. The often muddy path leads, eventually, to Delacorse hamlet. It passes the entrance portico and steps to Glan-y-Môr, incongruously grand in the overgrown setting.

THE 'BOAT HOUSE' TO ST MARTIN'S CHURCH

The left turn at the top of the 'Boat House' steps leads back into Laugharne. At the junction of Victoria Street and King Street is the Three Mariners pub. Thomas doubtless drank here now and again; we know that Kingsley Amis did. Though some romantics believe that King Street got its name because Henry II once passed this way to Laugharne Castle, in the Corporation records it is, more prosaically, 'Uptown Street'.

To the left of the junction was 'Manchester House', now closed but once a general store that latterly sold Dylan Thomas books and other material. Some suggest this was the model for Mr Mog Edwards's draper's emporium in *Under Milk Wood.* It is, though, worth remembering that New Quay also had its 'Manchester House', in Margaret Street, which is mentioned in 'Quite Early One Morning'. Almost immediately ahead of the junction with Victoria Street is *Corran Books.* The business is owned by the Tremletts, George Tremlett being the author of biographical studies of Thomas, and the editor of Caitlin Thomas's memoirs. They keep a marvellously old-fashioned bookshop, always capable of surprising the browser. Some of its books are new, most are second-hand; it specializes, as one might expect, in Dylan Thomas material and Welsh writing in English generally.

Opposite *Corran Books* is Brown's Hotel, Thomas's favourite Laugharne pub. A walk to 'moulder in Brown's' was part of his daily routine. In his day, as has been said, it was owned and kept by the ubiquitous – in Laugharne, at any rate – Ebie and Ivy Williams, those two generous friends. Sometimes Caitlin went with him, although she was known to complain about the hours he spent in pubs. He used the bar on the right as the visitor enters, often sitting in the window-seat playing cards with Ebie and Ivy. Sometimes – probably after hours – he would sit in the kitchen sharing gossip with the Williamses and betting on horses. Thomas's letters of the 'Boat House' years include much of this chat, in some instances reordered into neatly pointed sequences. *Under Milk Wood* is one consequence – sadly the only consequence – of this fascination with the drama and humour of everyday life. Brown's has its regulars and frequent visitors. Though it has been refurbished since Thomas drank its beer, it still has some atmosphere. A photograph on the wall once showed Dylan and Caitlin sitting at what could well be the very table – it is certainly the same style – on which until recently , the modern visitor, including the present writer, could place his or her drink. The old furniture was taken by a previous owner.

Opposite Brown's are two tall Georgian houses; the right-hand one, now refurbished, was once called 'The Pelican'. The name-plate was removed during a recent renovation. The house was once owned by Ebie Williams, from whom, in May 1949, Thomas rented the ground-floor flat for his aged parents. The rent was invariably late, Ebie invariably indulgent. Dylan, once the difficult boy and a worry to his parents, became the dutiful son. He visited most mornings and, as has been suggested, some afternoons, usually to chat and complete the crossword with his father, or to take him across the road for a pint of beer. But the once volatile and intellectually sharp D.J. became very infirm. 'Do not go gentle' dates mainly from this time, being completed in 1951 and published in *Botteghe Oscure* in November 1951. It was never shown to D.J. Though in sad decline he lived just long enough to see his son acclaimed for *Collected Poems 1934–1952*. He died, aged seventy-six, on 16 December 1952, within a month of that publication, and was cremated at Pontypridd. Thomas wrote movingly to Alfred Janes that his father 'was in awful pain at the end and nearly blind', and wrote of him hallucinating that he was a boy again and wanting his mother's onion soup. 'It's full circle now', said D.J., and died.

Dylan Thomas followed him less than a year later. When the embalmed body came back to Laugharne, the American-style casket was too large for the 'Boat House'. It was also too large for The Pelican's front door and corridor and, in order for it to be laid out in the front room in the traditional Welsh way, the casket was put through one of The Pelican's front windows. It was brought back out the same way on 24 November 1953, when Thomas was buried in Laugharne churchyard after a large funeral attended by his old friends and a number of famous writers. It was a day of much drinking and some wild behaviour.

Before reaching the church, King Street becomes Clifton Street. On the left-hand side is the vicarage and the 'Great House' where, as some have said, Mary Shelley once stayed, and then the vicarage. The old and rather down-at-heel town hall is further along Clifton Street. Here, as has been noted, during a BBC broadcast, Caitlin received news of her husband's death. A new hall, built to celebrate the Millennium, is alongside. Only a few yards further on is the parish church of St Martin of Tours, probably the 'sea wet church the size of a snail' glimpsed from a distance in 'Poem in October'.

As the name suggests, this is a Norman foundation, dating from the thirteenth century, dedicated to the great medieval ecclesiastic who founded the famous monastery at Tours in the Loire valley. The most famous of its many incumbents and curates was Griffith Jones (1683–1761) who, as an active member of the Society for Promoting Christian Knowledge, established circulating schools that made a tremendous contribution to the spread of literacy and knowledge of Christian principles. In the opinion of many, he was the greatest Welshman of the eighteenth century. The Most Reverend Derrick Childs, who became archbishop of Wales, served the parish as an assistant curate from 1946 to 1951.

The church was much restored in 1855 and again in 1873. The interior, though perhaps over-restored, is still attractive. For such a small and out-of-the-way place there are an unusual number of fine wall monuments. These include a memorial to Dylan Thomas, a replica of that placed in Poets' Corner in Westminster Abbey. The old churchyard, visited by Coleridge in 1802, has a number of family vaults and is unusual in being multilevelled.

Thomas, brought up a Nonconformist, as an adult rarely attended chapel, let alone church. One incumbent was fond of surprising many visitors by stating that Thomas was seen in church quite frequently. He hastened to say that, in the days of unlocked churches, the poet was prone to wander in during a walk after lunchtime drinking, and fall asleep on one of the rear pews. That said, the Thomases had at least one child, Llewelyn, baptized in St Martin's.

Dylan Thomas is buried in the new graveyard, over the bridge at the top of the steps from the church car park. A grassy track leads up the hill and then right to where the grave is marked by a plain white cross – for many years a wooden one, now uPVC – which stands out among the expensive gravestones. At first there was little to mark the grave, mainly because Caitlin wished to remove her husband's body for burial in the 'Boat House' garden. She obtained Home Office permission to do this but, by then, had left Laugharne for Italy and a new relationship, and had lost interest in the project. Following her death in Sicily on 31 July 1994, her wish to be buried with Dylan was honoured on 10 August 1994, when she was interred in the same grave. Her inscription is on the rear of the cross.

A few yards below the Thomases' grave, on the right, is the grave of Ebie and Ivy Williams 'of Brown's Hotel', also buried together. Here, in this peaceful place, a world away from roistering circumstance, the Laugharne he knew lies 'enfolded in a single party'. His work, of course, does not. As Dylan Thomas wrote, at that time hopefully and prophetically, at the close of his last completed poem:

> My ark sings in the sun
> At God speeded summer's end
> And the flood flowers now.

Further Reading

DYLAN THOMAS'S WORKS

Under Milk Wood. Preface by Daniel Jones (1954; Dent/Everyman, 1992).

Poet in the Making: The Notebooks of Dylan Thomas, ed. Ralph Maud (Dent, 1968).

Early Prose Writings, ed. Walford Davies (Dent, 1971).

The Poems, ed. Daniel Jones, revised edn (Dent 1982).

Collected Stories, ed. Walford Davies (1983; Dent/Everyman, 1995).

The Collected Letters, ed. Paul Ferris, revised edn (1985; Dent, 2000).

Collected Poems 1934–1953, ed. Walford Davies and Ralph Maud (Dent, 1988).

The Notebook Poems, 1930–34, ed. Ralph Maud (Dent, 1989).

The Broadcasts, ed. Ralph Maud (Dent, 1991).

The Filmscripts, ed. John Ackerman (Dent, 1995).

Under Milk Wood, 'The Definitive Edition', ed. Walford Davies and Ralph Maud (Dent, 1995).

Dylan Thomas, Poems Selected (and Introduced) by Derek Mahon (Faber and Faber, 2004).

GENERAL

Ackerman, John, *Dylan Thomas: His Life and Work* (1964; Macmillan, 1991).

—, *Welsh Dylan* (1979; Seren, 1998).

Avent, Richard, *Laugharne Castle* (Cadw, 1995).

Davies, James A., 'A picnic in the orchard: Dylan Thomas's Wales', *Wales: The Imagined Nation*, ed. Tony Curtis (Poetry Wales Press, 1986), pp. 45–65.

—, *Dylan Thomas's Places* (Christopher Davies, 1987).
—, *A Swansea Anthology* (1996; Seren, 1998).
—, *A Reference Companion to Dylan Thomas* (Greenwood Press, 1998).
Ellis, Aeronwy Thomas, *Later Than Laugharne* (Celtion Publications, 1976).
Ferris, Paul, *Caitlin: The Life of Caitlin Thomas* (Hutchinson, 1993).
—, *Dylan Thomas: The Biography*, new edn (Dent, 1999).
Fitzgibbon, Constantine, *Dylan Thomas* (Dent, 1965).
Fryer, Jonathan, *Dylan The Nine Lives of Dylan Thomas* (Kyle Cathie, 1993).
Goodby, John and Wigginton, Chris, *Dylan Thomas (New Casebooks)* (Palgrave, 2001).
Griffiths, Ralph A. (ed.), *The City of Swansea: Challenges and Change* (Alan Sutton, 1990).
Hughes, Beryl, *Dylan Thomas: The Final Story* (Beryl Hughes, 1998).
Hughes, Lynn (ed.), *A Carmarthenshire Anthology* (Christopher Davies, 1984).
Jones, Daniel, *My Friend Dylan Thomas* (Dent, 1977).
Lewis, Min, *Laugharne and Dylan Thomas* (Dobson, 1967).
Lycett, Andrew, *Dylan Thomas: A New Life* (Weidenfeld & Nicolson, 2003).
Maud, Ralph (ed.), *Dylan Thomas in Print* (Dent, 1970).
—, *Wales in His Arms: Dylan Thomas's Choice of Welsh Poetry* (University of Wales Press, 1994).
__, *Where Have the Old Words Got Me?* (University of Wales Press, 2003).
Read, Bill, *The Days of Dylan Thomas* (Weidenfeld & Nicolson, 1965).
Scourfield, Lorraine, *The Dylan Thomas Boat House Laugharne: Official Guidebook* (Carmarthen District Council, n.d.).
Sinclair, Andrew, *Dylan Thomas: Poet of his People* (Michael Joseph, 1975).
Stead, Peter, 'The Swansea of Dylan Thomas', *Dylan Thomas Remembered* (The Dylan Thomas Society Wales Branch, 1978), pp. 8–25.
Thomas, Caitlin, with Tremlett, George, *Caitlin: A Warring Absence* (Secker & Warburg, 1986).
Thomas, David N., *Dylan Thomas: A Farm, Two Mansions and a Bungalow* (Seren, 2000).
Tremlett, George, *Dylan Thomas: In the Mercy of his Means* (Constable, 1991).
Watkins, Gwen, *Portrait of a Friend* (Gomer Press, 1983).
Watkins, Vernon, *Collected Poems* (Golgonooza Press, 1986).
Williams, Glanmor (ed.), *Swansea: An Illustrated History* (Christopher Davies, 1990).

Index

(For all locations in Swansea, Gower and Laugharne, look under the respective entries for those places. All references to Dylan Thomas's works will be found under Thomas Dylan Marlais)

Index

Index

Index

Index